THE INFLUENCES OF
LUCIFER AND AHRIMAN

THE INFLUENCES OF LUCIFER AND AHRIMAN

Human Responsibility for the Earth

Five lectures given by Rudolf Steiner in November, 1919
from shorthand reports unrevised by the lecturer
Translated by D. S. Osmond

RUDOLF STEINER

✑ ANTHROPOSOPHIC PRESS

Lectures I, II, IV, and V of this book are translations of lectures Eleven (November 1, 1919), Twelve (November 2, 1919), Fifteen (November 15, 1919) and Thirteen (November 9, 1919) of *Soziales Verständnis aus geisteswissenschaftlicher Erkenntnis*. *Die geistigen Hintergründe der sozialen Frage*, which is volume 191 [GA191] in the Collected Works of Rudolf Steiner, published by the Rudolf Steiner Verlag, Dornach, Switzerland, 1972; Lecture III of this book is a translation of Lecture Ten (November 4, 1919) of *Der innere Aspekt des sozialen Rätsels*. *Luziferische Vergangenheit und ahrimanische Zukunft*, which is volume 193 [GA193] of the Collected Works of Rudolf Steiner, published by the Rudolf Steiner Verlag, Dornach, Switzerland, 1977.

First published in English by Rudolf Steiner Publishing Co. 1954
Second and Third impressions by Steiner Book Centre, Inc, N. Vancouver, 1976 and 1984

Translation by permission of the Rudolf Steiner
Nachlassverwaltung, Dornach, Switzerland
Translated by D. S. Osmond

Revised Translation © 1993 Anthroposophic Press

Published by Anthroposophic Press, Inc.

Library of Congress Cataloging-in-Publication Data

Steiner, Rudolf, 1861-1925.
The influences of Lucifer and Ahriman : human responsibility for the Earth : five lectures given by Rudolf Steiner in November, 1919 / Rudolf Steiner ; translated from shorthand reports unrevised by the lecturer by D.S. Osmond.
    p. cm.
ISBN 0-88010-375-2 (pbk.)
1. Devil. 2. Angra Mainyu. 3. Anthroposophy. I. Title.
BP595.S894I5413 1993
299′ .935—dc20
                                                                        93-546
                                                                        CIP

CONTENTS

INTRODUCTION

HUMAN BEINGS ARE DWELLERS in two worlds. Our uniqueness amongst the creatures of the earth lies in this role that we have as half beast and half angel. A dynamic tension exists because of the contrary demands which living in each of these realms places on us. We experience this on a daily basis, an internal tug-of-war, pulling first in one direction, then to the opposite pole. Whenever we are called upon to make a choice, a decision, the earthly and the heavenly draw us one way or the other and often both at once!

A long held view has been that, of course, one should always give way to the heavenly or spiritual; the alternative is to succumb to the earthly, the fallen, to evil. The struggle has been portrayed as white versus black, as good versus evil. The enduring legacy of this attitude has been to deem the earthly, the bodily nature of the human being as soiled, unclean, corrupt, shameful. With this view the spiritual aspirant of the past had no choice but to reject the body, the earth. In India incarnating into a physical body has long been considered a curse, the entering into the "veil of tears" which constitutes life.

The physical body was especially singled out for punishment, to be starved and tortured, purged and scourged. St. Francis derided his body as his "donkey", but reluctantly acknowledged that he must give it some care if it was to continue carrying him about. The medieval Cathars saw the human body as a pit into which the devil had lured the souls of weakened angels. Procreation was thus looked upon with horror as an act of unwitting cruelty—each new birth dragged a heavenly soul into the fallen world of matter, bringing another diabolically corrupt angel into the flesh. Even to study the physical body too closely was suspect, hence Leonardo's need for secrecy in dissection of corpses. The accumulation of an inordinate amount of the material realm in the form of wealth has also been rather suspect.

Such views have persisted on varying levels into modern times, and not just amongst the puritanical or the late Victorian. Sigmund Freud had difficulty, as a scientist, in acknowledging an angelic side in his patients. He reframed the conflict as one involving human bodily nature and the probably superstitious religious and moral beliefs they maintain. This wrestling match between the instinctual id and the moralistic superego was refereed by the central ego.

Later psychologists have continued to use this framework of two opposing forces moderated by the central force of an ego (though they all interpret the ego somewhat difflerently). Gestalt psychologists very pragmatically focus on how an individual becomes caught in this struggle between the two poles, without worrying about the relative merits of either pole— what is important is to get the individual "unstuck", to empower the central ego to again be able to choose, to act more decisively through becoming conscious of its dilemma. The Italian psychiatrist, Robert Assagioli, wrote of the pull between the lower and higher unconscious, once again recognizing an earth/heaven dichotomy. He developed a therapy that sought a "psychosynthesis" of the two opposing forces, paving the way for the discovery of one's unifying center. Similarly, Carl Jung described the marriage of Eros and Logos within the soul, with the sometimes alchemical participation of the ego.

Some of these more spiritually inclined psychologists share with Rudolf Steiner the recognition that it is a synthesis of the two poles and not the choosing of one over the other that frees us for self-development. Humanity has both an earthly and a heavenly mission, tasks in the outer world as well as the inner, necessitating an acceptance, an embracing of both our natures.

In examining this predicament of living in two worlds, Rudolf Steiner, by virtue of his capacity for spiritual research, went much further than previous researchers. Steiner was able not merely to speak of opposing psychological forces, but to relate these specifically to the influence of mighty spiritual beings, Lucifer and Ahriman. The influence of these beings is not to be thought of as limited to the realm of the soul but rather taken in the widest context as encompassing human evolution, history, and almost every aspect of our existence.

The name Lucifer comes from the Latin meaning "bearer of the Light". One's childhood picture of Lucifer as a slithering manifestation of evil is difficult to reconcile with the beauty of this name. Lucifer, however, represents a force that paradoxically can combine beauty and if you will, beauty gone too far, to the extreme of decadence, hence to evil.

In the Greek legend, Icarus and his father Daedalus escape from the tower of their island prison with wings fashioned of wax. Despite his father's warning, Icarus becomes enamored of his newfound power and of the beauty of the Sun; he flies up to the light (and heat), his wings melt, and he falls to his death. The wiser and more restrained Daedalus keeps his flight balanced between heaven and earth, thus succeeding in his escape from bondage. The Greeks were very aware of the temptation of Lucifer—in most of their tales of tragedy, "hubris" or overweening pride was the source of a hero's downfall.

In Rudolf Steiner's sculpture, the *Representative of Humanity*, Lucifer is portrayed as an exceedingly handsome and powerful winged form. Despite his having fallen from Heaven, he was nevertheless, an angel, a leader of angels. As the Light Bearer he has particular gifts for humankind, especially that of wisdom, the gift he first offered to Adam and Eve. By their eating of the fruit of the Tree of Knowledge, Lucifer promised that they would "be as gods". Like Icarus, they were not yet prepared for such a gift and ignoring warnings to the contrary, they accepted it and fell from Paradise. In this example it should be noted that the gift in and of itself is not evil. As in our earlier psychological examples, neither the heavenly nor the earthly is of itself to be seen as either absolutely desirable or absolutely forbidden. The beings of the polarities actually have something of value to offer to humanity. This is very different from the traditional view of the Devil's offerings! However, an individual must be inwardly prepared for the reception of these gifts if they are to be of any value. The hallucinogenic drug user is open to receiving Luciferic light and often feels quite wise when in the midst of the drug experience. Without the meditative discipline of the serious student of the spirit, however, the contact with those realms is rarely beneficial and, in fact, is often quite harmful.

In this century, society has especially interested itself in the material. Partially in response to the excessive rejection of the earth and the body, and of the authoritarianism which maintained this position, we have now fully entered the realm of matter, with head, heart, and soul. Whereas in former times humankind was more dreamy in its consciousness and thus more prone to the Luciferic realm of fantasy, illusion, and superstitious thinking, modern consciousness tends to the concrete, to materialism. The belief only in what can be ascertained by the physical senses (and the instruments which extend those senses) binds us to the earth and to the influence of the being named Ahriman.

Aingra Mainu, or Ahriman, was first spoken of in the Zoroastrianism of ancient Persia. He was the evil god, the lord of lies who tempted men and women to believe that they were solely earthly beings. At a time in history when the clairvoyance which had once been common was becoming rare, the ethical teachings of Zarathustra sought to remind the people of their divine origin and to teach through the revelation he had received of the Lord of the Sun, Ahura Mazda.

The influence of Ahriman has grown through the centuries, quietly gaining respectability in the age of the Renaissance and flourishing in our own century as *the* predominant worldview. Only in the last years has there been any serious questioning of the notion that the only reality is the physical one. For the most part the realm of soul and spirit has been dismissed. The prevailing scientific view has been that only what can be weighed, measured, or quantified should merit serious attention. Ahriman has welcomed statistics as his handmaid.

At the beginning of the century, the Russian philosopher, Vladimir Soloviev, warned of this danger in his "A Short Narrative about Anti-Christ". In this fictional essay Soloviev described the appearance of a great individual who taught world peace and became first the World Leader, and later the reuniter of the world's religions. He is a vegetarian and anti-vivisectionist and brings great material prosperity and physical comfort to all who acknowledge his authority, all of this without effort on the people's part. The world becomes peaceful, even docile, for the minor sacrifice of individuality and freedom.

The influence of Ahriman is seen in the generous gifts that he has bestowed on humankind in the past centuries and for which we must feel very grateful. All of the technological marvels which science has made possible have given many of us relative freedom from all manner of drudgery while maintaining a high standard of living, freeing us to pursue other interests, giving us more time...or do we have more time? The great difficulty with our acceptance of Ahriman's bounty has been our relative blindness and lack of foresight as we have lost ourselves in its enjoyment. The birth of the ecology movement and discussion of the reductionist nature of science has wakened some consciousness of the danger into which we have strayed. Some awareness has arisen as to what we are sacrificing in the Faustian bargain which society has struck, a sacrifice which involves our very humanity.

Through Darwin's theory of evolution as well as through Freud's positing of the sexual as the primary motive of humankind, the idea that we are no more than "naked apes" has become quite accepted. To this instinctual or animalistic picture of the human, science has added the model of the human being as machine, with the brain as computer. With such a confining definition of humanity, is it any wonder that we have increasingly come to act and to see ourselves as just machines, or just animals?

The challenge for the individual is often not how to face either Ahriman or Lucifer, but how not to be torn asunder in the encounter with both forces. In T.S. Eliot's play, *Murder in the*

Cathedral, the Archbishop of Canterbury, Thomas á Becket, is conducted to an examination of himself and his past by a succession of four Tempters. The first three attempt to win him with the Ahrimanic enticements of pleasures of the senses, good fellowship, and temporal power for himself and for his Church. Becket turns away from these three only to be approached by a fourth Tempter, clad like himself as a priest and tonsured. The Luciferic temptation now offered is the most dangerous and difficult for Becket, the whisper of spiritual pride—to die in order to attain immortality on earth, to envisage the saint's tomb being visited by pilgrims for centuries, to stand high within the ranks in heaven. Only with difficulty does Becket turn away from these "higher vices".

In Rudolf Steiner's sculpture, a strong figure stands with one clenched hand upraised to the beautiful Lucifer, the other hand stretched downward to the twisted and sclerotic Ahriman. *The Representative of Humanity* stands heroically, holding at bay and in balance the two opposing forces, centered within the "Third Force", that force which we recognize in ourselves in the word "I".

In this series of lectures, Rudolf Steiner strives to deepen our understanding of the two opposing forces, to alert us especially to the dangers of Ahriman, whose wiles have lulled us into a soporific state. The intent, however, is not to drive us to obsession over Luciferic or Ahrimanic demons, but rather to remind us, to reawaken us to our true center. In the words of Henry David Thoreau, "We must learn to reawaken and keep ourselves awake, not by mechanical means, but by an infinite expectation of the dawn, which does not forsake us even in our soundest sleep." We recognize that dawn in the figure of the risen Christ who stands for all of us as the "Representative of Humanity" in the modern struggle for the kernel of our being.

Thomas Poplawski

LECTURE ONE

WHEN SOCIAL QUESTIONS are discussed from a spiritual scientific point of view, this is not done out of any subjective motive or impulse. Everything is based upon observation of the evolution of humanity and of what the forces underlying that evolution demand of us now and in the immediate future.

To reveal the deeper impulses working at the present time is not a congenial task, for there is little inclination to enter into such matters with any real earnestness. But our age calls for this earnestness wherever the affairs of humanity are concerned, above all for the discarding of prejudices and preconceptions. Today, therefore, I shall put before you certain deeper aspects of matters to which reference has often been made.

Once again it is necessary to survey a rather lengthy period in the life of humanity. As you know, we distinguish the present epoch from other epochs, reckoning that it began in the middle of the fifteenth century A.D. We speak of it as the fifth post-Atlantean epoch, distinguishing it from the previous epoch which began in the eighth century B.C. and is called the Greco-Latin epoch after the peoples responsible for its culture. It was preceded by the epoch of Egypto-Chaldean civilization.

When we come to consider the Egypto-Chaldean epoch we find that the records of ordinary history break down. Even with the help of accessible Egyptian and Chaldean lore, external evidence does not carry us very far back in the history of humanity.

But it is not possible to grasp what is of importance for the present time unless we understand the intrinsic characteristics of that third post-Atlantean epoch of culture.

You are certainly aware that in the ordinary history of that ancient time, all civilization, all culture in the then-known world, goes by the name of paganism. Like an oasis, Hebraic culture arises in its midst as a preparation for Christianity. But disregarding for the moment this Jewish culture which differed so fundamentally from the other forms of pre-Christian civilized life, let us turn our attention to paganism. Its special characteristic may be said to lie in its wisdom, in its deep insight into the things and processes of the world. The knowledge contained in paganism had its source in the ancient Mysteries and although according to modern scholarship it bears a mythical, pictorial character, it must be emphasized that all the imagery, all the pictures which have come down to posterity from this ancient paganism are the fruits of profound insight.

Recalling the many treasures of this supersensible lore which we have been endeavoring to bring to light, it will be obvious that here we have to do with a primeval wisdom, a wisdom underlying all the thinking, all the perceptions and feelings of those ancient peoples. A kind of echo of this primeval wisdom, a tradition in which it was enshrined, survived here and there in secret societies, actually in a healthy form, until the end of the eighteenth century and at the beginning of the nineteenth. In the nineteenth century the source ran dry and such vestiges as remain have passed into the hands of isolated groups belonging to certain nationalities. And what is in the possession of ordinary secret societies today can no longer be regarded as wholesome or as a genuine tradition of the old pagan wisdom.

Now this ancient wisdom has one particular characteristic of which sight must never be lost. It has one characteristic on account of which Judaism, the smaller stream then making preparation for Christianity, had to be introduced as a kind of oasis.

If this ancient paganism is rightly understood, it will be found to contain sublime, deeply penetrating wisdom, but no *moral impulses* for human action. These impulses were not really essential to humanity, for unlike what now passes as human knowledge, human insight, this old pagan wisdom gave one the feeling of being membered into the whole cosmos. People moving about the earth not only felt themselves composed of the substances and forces present around them in earthly life, in the mineral, plant, and animal kingdoms, but they felt that the forces operating, for example, in the movements of the stars and the sun were playing into them. This feeling of being a member of the whole cosmos was not a mere abstraction, for from the Mysteries they received directives based on the laws of the stars for their actions and whole conduct of life. This ancient star-wisdom was in no way akin to the arithmetical astrology sometimes considered valuable today, but it was a wisdom voiced by the initiates in such a way that impulses for individual action and conduct went forth from the Mysteries. Not only did human beings feel safe and secure within the all-prevailing wisdom of the cosmos, but those whom they recognized as the initiates of the Mysteries imparted this wisdom in directives for their actions from morning till evening on given days of the year. Yet neither Chaldean nor Egyptian wisdom contained a single moral impulse from what had been imparted by the initiates in this way. The moral impulse in its real sense was prepared by Judaism and then further developed in Christianity.

Inevitably the question arises: Why is it that this sublime pagan wisdom, although it contained no moral impulse, was able, for example in ancient Greece, to come to flower in such beauty of art and grandeur of philosophy?

If we were to go much farther back, to a time more than three thousand years before the Christian era, we should find that together with the promptings of wisdom there *did* come a moral impulse, that the moral principles, the ethics needed by these people of old were contained in this wisdom. But a specific *ethos*, a specific moral impulse such as came with

Christianity was not an integral part of paganism. Why was this? It was because through the millennia directly preceding Christianity, this pagan wisdom was inspired from a place far away in Asia, inspired by a remarkable being who had been incarnated in the distant East in the third millennium before Christ—namely, Lucifer.

To the many things we have learned about the evolution of humanity, this knowledge too must be added: that just as there was the incarnation which culminated in Golgotha, the incarnation of Christ in the man Jesus of Nazareth, there was an actual incarnation of Lucifer in far-off Asia, in the third millennium B.C. And the source of inspiration for much ancient culture was what can only be described as an earthly incarnation of Lucifer in a man of flesh and blood. Even Christianity, even the Mystery of Golgotha as enacted among human beings, was understood at first by the only means then available, namely the old luciferic wisdom. The onesidedness of the gnosis, for all its amazing profundity, stems from the influence that had spread from this Lucifer incarnation over the whole of the ancient world. The significance of the Mystery of Golgotha cannot be fully grasped without the knowledge that rather less than three thousand years previously, there had been the incarnation of Lucifer.

In order that the luciferic inspiration might be lifted away from its onesidedness, there came the incarnation of Christ and with it the impulse for the education and development of European civilization and its American offshoot. But since the middle of the fifteenth century, since the impulse for the development of individuality, of personality, has been at work, this phase of evolution has also contained within it certain forces whereby preparation is being made for the incarnation of another supersensible Being. Just as there was an incarnation of Lucifer in the flesh and an incarnation of Christ in the flesh, so, before only a part of the third millennium of the post-Christian era has elapsed, there will be, in the West, an actual incarnation of Ahriman: Ahriman in the flesh. Humanity on earth cannot escape this incarnation of Ahriman. It will come inevitably. But what matters is that people shall find the right vantage point from which to confront it.

Whenever preparation is being made for incarnations of this character, we must be alert to certain indicative trends in evolution. A being like Ahriman, who will incarnate in the West in time to come, prepares for this incarnation in advance. With a view to his incarnation on the earth, Ahriman guides certain forces in evolution in such a way that they may be of the greatest possible advantage to him. And evil would result were people to live on in a state of drowsy unawareness, unable to recognize certain phenomena in life as preparations for Ahriman's incarnation in the flesh. The right stand can be taken only by recognizing in one or another series of events the preparation that is being made by Ahriman for his earthly existence. And the time has now come for individual human beings to know what tendencies and events around them are machinations of Ahriman, helping him to prepare for his approaching incarnation.

It would undoubtedly be of the greatest benefit to Ahriman if he could succeed in preventing the vast majority of people from perceiving what would make for their true well-being, if the vast majority of people were to regard these preparations for the Ahriman incarnation as progressive and good for evolution. If Ahriman were able to slink into a humanity unaware of his coming, that would gladden him most of all. It is for this reason that the occurrences and trends in which Ahriman is working for his future incarnation must be brought to light.

One of the developments in which Ahriman's impulse is clearly evident is the spread of the belief that the mechanistic, mathematical conceptions inaugurated by Galileo, Copernicus, and others, explain what is happening in the cosmos. That is why anthroposophical spiritual science lays such stress upon the fact that *spirit* and *soul* must be discerned in the cosmos, not merely the mathematical, mechanistic laws put forward by Galileo and Copernicus as if the cosmos were some huge machine. It would augur success for Ahriman's temptings if people were to persist in merely calculating the revolutions of the heavenly bodies, in studying astro physics for the sole purpose of ascertaining the material composition of the planets— an achievement of which the modern world is so proud. But woe betide if this Copernicanism is not confronted by the knowledge that the cosmos is permeated by soul and spirit. It is this knowledge that Ahriman, in preparing his earthly incarnation, wants to withhold. He would like to keep people so obtuse that they can grasp only the mathematical aspect of astronomy. Therefore he tempts many people to carry into effect their repugnance to knowledge concerning soul and spirit in the cosmos. That is only *one* of the forces of corruption poured by Ahriman into human souls. Another means of temptation connected with his incarnation—he also works in cooperation with the luciferic forces—another of his endeavors is to preserve the already widespread attitude that for the public welfare it is sufficient if the economic and material needs of humanity are provided for. Here we come to a point that is not willingly faced in modern life. Official science nowadays contributes nothing to real knowledge of the soul and spirit, for the methods adopted in the orthodox sciences are of value only for apprehending external nature, including the external human constitution. Just think with what contempt average citizens today regard anything that seems idealistic, anything that seems to be a path leading in any way to the spiritual. At heart they are always asking: What is the good of it? How will it help me to acquire this world's goods? They send their sons to a private school, having perhaps been to one themselves; they send them on to a university or institute of advanced studies. But all this is done merely in order to provide the foundations for a career, in other words, to provide the material means of livelihood.

And now think of the consequences of this. What numbers of people there are today who no longer value the spirit for the sake of the spirit or the soul for the sake of the soul! They are out to absorb from cultural life only what is regarded as "useful." This is a significant and mysterious factor in the life of modern humanity and one that must be lifted into the full light of consciousness. Average citizens who work assiduously in their offices from morning till evening and then go through the habitual evening routine, will not allow themselves to get mixed up with what they call the "twaddle" to be found in anthroposophy. It seems to them entirely redundant, for they think: that is something one cannot eat! It finally comes to this—although people will not admit it—that in ordinary life nothing in the way of knowledge is considered really useful unless it helps to put food in the mouth!

In this connection people today have succumbed to a strange fallacy. They do not believe that the spirit can be eaten, and yet the very ones who say this, *do* eat the spirit! Although they may refuse to accept anything spiritual, nevertheless with every morsel that passes through the mouth into the stomach they are devouring the spiritual, but dispatching it along a path other than the path which leads to the real well-being of mankind.

I believe that many Europeans think it is to the credit of their civilization to be able to say: We are not cannibals! But these Europeans and their American affinities are, none the less, devourers of soul and spirit! The soulless devouring of material food leads to the side-tracking of the spirit. It is difficult to say these things today, for in the light of such knowledge just think what would have to be said of a large section of modern culture! To keep people in the state of being devourers of the soul and spirit is one of Ahriman's impulses in preparation for his incarnation. To the extent to which people can be roused into conducting their affairs not for material ends alone and into regarding a free and independent spiritual life, equally with economic life, as an integral part of the social organism—to that same extent Ahriman's incarnation will be awaited with an attitude worthy of humanity.

Another tendency in modern life of benefit to Ahriman in preparing his incarnation is all that is so clearly in evidence in *nationalism.* Whatever can separate people into groups, whatever can alienate them from mutual understanding the whole world over and drive wedges between them, strengthens Ahriman's impulse. In reality we should recognize the voice of Ahriman in what is so often proclaimed nowadays as a new ideal: "Freedom of the peoples, even the smallest," and so forth. But blood relationship has ceased to be the decisive factor and if this outworn notion persists, we shall be playing straight into the hands of Ahriman. His interests are promoted, too, by the fact that people are taken up with the most divergent shades of party opinions, of which the one can be justified as easily as the other. A socialist party program and an anti-socialist program can be supported by arguments of equal validity. And if people fail to realize that this kind of "proof" lies so utterly on the surface that the No and the Yes can both be justified with our modern intelligence—useful as it is for natural science but not for a different kind of knowledge—if people do not realize that this intelligence lies entirely on the surface in spite of serving economic life so effectively, they will continue to apply it to social life and spiritual life irrespectively. One group will prove one thing, another its exact opposite, and as both proofs can be shown to be equally logical, hatred and bitterness—of which there is more than enough in the world—will be intensified. These trends too are exploited by Ahriman in preparation for his earthly incarnation.

Again, what will be of particular advantage to him is the short-sighted, narrow conception of the Gospel that is so prevalent today. You know how necessary it has become in our time to deepen understanding of the Gospels through spiritual science. But you also know how widespread is the notion that this is not fitting, that it is reprehensible to bring any real knowledge of the spirit or of the cosmos to bear upon the Gospels; it is said that the Gospels must be taken "in all their simplicity," just as they stand. I am not going to raise the issue that we no longer possess the *true* Gospels. The translations are not faithful reproductions of the authentic Gospels, but I do not propose to go into this question now. I shall merely put before you the deeper fact, namely that no true understanding of Christ can be reached by the simple, easy going perusal of the Gospels beloved by most religious denominations and sects today. At the time of the Mystery of Golgotha and for a few centuries afterward, a conception of the real Christ was still possible, because accounts handed down by tradition could be understood with the help of the pagan, luciferic wisdom. This wisdom has now disappeared, and what sects and denominations find in the Gospels does not lead people to the real Christ for whom we seek through spiritual science, but to an illusory picture, at most to a sublimated hallucination of Christ.

The Gospels cannot lead to the real Christ unless they are illumined by spiritual science. Failing this illumination, the Gospels as they stand give rise to what is no more than hallucination of Christ's appearance in world history. This becomes very evident in the theology of our time. Why does modern theology so love to speak of the "simple man of Nazareth" and to identify the Christ with Jesus of Nazareth—whom it regards as a man only a little more exalted than other great figures of history? It is because the possibility of finding the real Christ has been lost, and because what people glean from the Gospels leads to hallucination, to a kind of illusion. An illusory conception of Christ is all that can be gleaned through the way in which the Gospels are read today—not the *reality* of Christ. In a certain sense this has actually dawned on the theologians and many of them are now describing Paul's experience on the way to Damascus as a "vision." They have come to the point of realizing that their way of studying the Gospels can lead only to a vision, to hallucination. I am not saying that this vision is false or untrue, but that it is merely an *inner* experience, unconnected with the reality of the Christ being. I do not use the word "illusion" with the side-implication of falsity, but I wish only to stress that the Christ Being is here a subjective, inner experience, of the same character as hallucination. If people could be brought to a standstill at this point, not pressing on to the real Christ but contenting themselves with an hallucination of Christ, Ahriman's aims would be immeasurably furthered.

The influence of the Gospels also leads to hallucinations when *one* Gospel alone is taken as the basis of belief. Truth to tell, this principle has been forestalled by the fact that we have been given *four* Gospels, representing four different aspects, and it does not do to take each single Gospel word-for-word on its own, when outwardly there are obvious contradictions. To take one single Gospel word-for-word and disregard the other three is actually dangerous. What you find in sects whose adherents swear by the literal content of the Gospel of St. Luke alone or that of St. John alone is an illusory conception arising from a certain dimming of consciousness. With the dimming of consciousness that inevitably occurs when the deeper content of the Gospels is not revealed, people would fall wholly into Ahriman's service, helping in a most effective way to prepare for his incarnation, and adopting toward him the very attitude he desires.

And now another uncomfortable truth for humankind today! Living in the arms of their denominations, people say: "We do not need anthroposophy or anything of the kind; we are content with the Gospels in all their simplicity." They insist that this is said out of "humility." In reality, however, it is the greatest arrogance! For it means that such persons, making use of ideas which have been presented to them through their birth and surge out of their blood, are deigning to rule out the deeper treasures of wisdom to be discovered in the Gospels. These "humblest" of human beings are generally the most arrogant of all, especially in the sects and denominations. The point to remember is, however, that the people who do most to prepare for the incarnation of Ahriman are those who constantly preach: "All that is required is to read the Gospels word-for-word—nothing more than that!"

Strange to say, in spite of their radical differences, the two parties play into each other's hands: those whom I called "devourers of soul and spirit" and those who demand the literal, word-for-word reading of the Gospels. Each party plays into the hands of the other, furthering the preparation of Ahriman's incarnation. For if the outlook of the "devourers of soul and spirit" on the one side and that of professed Christians who refuse to enter into the deeper truths of the Gospels on the other were to hold the day, then Ahriman would be able to make all human beings on the earth his own. A good deal of what is spreading in external Christianity today is a preparation for Ahriman's incarnation. And in many things which arrogantly claim to represent true belief, we should recognize the preparation for Ahriman's work.

Words nowadays do not really convey the innermost reality of things. As I have often told you, far too much store is set upon words—for words do not necessarily lead to that reality; nowadays indeed it is rather a case of words separating people from the real nature of things in the world. And this they do most of all when people accept ancient records such as the Gospels with "simple understanding"—as the saying goes. But there is a far truer simplicity in trying to penetrate to the in dwelling spirit of things and to understand the Gospels themselves from the vantage ground of the spirit.

As I told you, Ahriman and Lucifer will always work hand in hand. The only question is which of the two predominates in human consciousness at a particular epoch of time. It was a preeminently luciferic culture that persisted until after the Mystery of Golgotha—a culture inspired by the incarnation of Lucifer in China in the third millennium B.C. Many influences of this incarnation continued to radiate and were still powerful in the early Christian centuries; indeed they are working to this day.

But now that we are facing an incarnation of Ahriman in the third millennium after Christ, Lucifer's tracks are becoming less visible, and Ahriman's activities in such trends as I have indicated are coming into prominence. Ahriman has made a kind of pact with Lucifer, the import of which may be expressed in the following way. Ahriman, speaking to Lucifer, says: "I, Ahriman, find it advantageous to make use of 'preserving jars.' To you I will leave people's stomachs, if you will leave it to me to lull them to sleep—that is to say to lull their consciousness to sleep where their stomachs are concerned."

You must understand what I mean by this. The consciousness of those human beings whom I have called devourers of soul and spirit is in a condition of dimness so far as their stomachs are concerned; for by not accepting the spiritual into their human nature, they drive straight into the luciferic stream everything they introduce into their stomachs. What people eat and drink without spirituality goes straight to Lucifer!

And what do I mean by "preserving jars"? I mean libraries and institutions of a similar kind, where the various sciences pursued by human beings without really stirring their interest are preserved; these sciences are not really alive in them but are simply preserved in the books on the shelves of libraries. All this knowledge has been separated from human beings. Everywhere there are books, books, books! Themselves students, when they take their doctor's degree, have to write a learned thesis which is then put into as many libraries as possible. When the students want to take up some particular post, again they must write a thesis! In addition to this, people are forever writing, although only a very small proportion of what they write is ever read. Only when some special preparation has to be made do people resort to what is moldering away in libraries. These "preserving jars" of wisdom are a particularly favorable means of furthering Ahriman's aims.

This kind of thing goes on everywhere. It could only be to some purpose if people took a really live interest in it, but they do not, its existence is entirely separate and apart. Just think— if one were so disposed one might well despair—just think, for example, of a lawsuit where a lawyer has to be engaged to plead the case. The time comes when one has to discuss the matter. Documents pile up! The lawyer has them all there in a dossier, but when one starts talking, this lawyer has no inkling of the circumstances. The papers are turned over and over without getting anywhere; the lawyer has no connection at all with the documents. Here is one portfolio full of them, there another. The number of documents grows and grows but as for interest in them—that is simply nonexistent! These professional people make one despair when one has dealings with them; they really know nothing about the matter at issue, have no connection with it, for everything remains in the documents. These are the little preserving jars and the libraries are the big preserving jars of soul and spirit. Everything is preserved in them but human beings do not want to connect themselves with it, to permeate it with their interest. And finally there arises the mood which does not want the head to play any part in a professed view of the world. But after all, the head, or some element of the head, is necessary for any understanding! What people like is to base their religious faith, their view of the world, on the heart alone. The heart must play a part, of course; but the way in which people today often speak of their religion reminds me of a saying much quoted in the district where my youth was spent. It was to this effect: "There is something very special about love. If you buy it, you buy the heart only and the head is thrown in gratis." This is more or less the attitude which people today like to adopt in their view of life; they would like to take in everything through the heart, as they say, without exerting the head at all. The heart cannot beat without the head, but the heart is well able to take things in if by "heart" here one really means the stomach! And then, what ought to be achieved through the head is supposed to be thrown in gratis, especially where the most important things in life are concerned. It is very important indeed to pay heed to these matters, because in observing them it becomes evident what earnestness must be applied to life at this juncture, how necessary it is to learn from the illusions to which even the Gospels may give rise, and how dearly humankind today loves those illusions.

Truth is beyond the reach of the kind of knowledge for which people aspire today. They feel on secure ground when they can reckon by means of figures, when they can prove things by statistics. With statistics and figures Ahriman has an easy game; it suits him admirably when some erudite scholar points out, for example, that conditions in the Balkans are due to the fact that the population of Macedonia consists of so many Greeks, so many Serbs, so many Bulgarians. Nothing can stand up against figures because of the faith that is reposed in them; and Ahriman is only too ready to exploit figures for his purposes. But later on one begins to see just how "reliable" such figures are! Admittedly, figures are sometimes a means of proof, but if one goes beyond them and investigates more closely, one often notices things like the following. In the statistics of Macedonia, for example, a father may be put down as a Greek, one son as a Serb, another son as a Bulgarian; so the father is counted in with the Greeks, one son with the Serbs, and the other with the Bulgarians. What would really help one to get at the truth, however, would be to discover how it has happened that in the same family one is said to be Greek, one Serbian, and one Bulgarian, and how this affects the figures— rather than simply accepting the figures that people find so satisfactory today. If the father is Greek then naturally the sons are Greek too. Figures are means whereby people are led astray in a direction favorable to Ahriman for his future incarnation in the third millennium A.D.

We shall speak of these things again in the lecture tomorrow.

LECTURE TWO

THE LECTURE YESTERDAY will have shown you that if we are to acquire insight into the nature and evolution of humanity, we must be constantly mindful of the power and influence of Lucifer, of Christ, and of Ahriman.

These influences were, of course, already at work in earlier stages of cosmic evolution, but in spheres where it was unnecessary for people to have clear consciousness of their effects. On the other hand, the very purpose of our fifth post-Atlantean epoch is that human beings should become increasingly conscious of what takes effect through them in earthly existence. The unveiling of many more of the secrets of human life would be desirable at the present time if only there were greater willingness to face things frankly and objectively. For without the knowledge of certain facts of the kind indicated yesterday, it will not be possible for humanity to make progress either in the inner life or in the sphere of social life. Think only of something that is connected with the social problems we have recently been studying. It has been our aim to demonstrate the necessity for separating the spiritual life, and also the political life or life of rights, from the economic life. Our greatest concern is to create conditions throughout the world, or at least—for we cannot do more at present—to convince people of the necessity for conditions which would provide the foundation for a free spiritual life no longer dependent upon the other spheres of social life or as deeply entangled as it is today in the economic life on the one side and in the political life of the state on the other. Civilized humankind must either establish the independence of the spiritual life or face collapse—with the inevitable result of an Asiatic influence taking effect in the future.

Those who still do not recognize the gravity of the present situation in the world are also, in a certain respect, helping to prepare for Ahriman's incarnation. Many things in external life today bear witness to this. The ahrimanic incarnation will be greatly furthered if people fail to establish a free and independent spiritual life and allow it to remain entangled in the economic or political life. For the ahrimanic power has everything to gain by the spiritual life being even more closely intermingled with these other spheres. To the ahrimanic power a free spiritual life would denote a kind of darkness, and people's interest in it, a burning, raging fire. The establishment of this free spiritual life is essential in order that the right attitude, the right relationship, may be adopted to Ahriman's incarnation in the future.

But there is still a strong tendency today to conceal the facts of which we spoke yesterday. The vast majority of people cast a veil over these things; they refuse to see them as they really are and allow themselves to be deceived by words which have no connection with reality. And very often, endeavors to shirk reality are described as "honest" and "well-meaning."

Take, for example, the recently published letter of Romain Rolland, in which he says that people should not allow themselves to be deluded by erstwhile proclamations of the victorious powers concerning justice and the upholding of political rights. The treatment which Russia is receiving from the Entente has led him to speak in these terms. He says: No matter whether it be on the part of monarchies or republics—what has been said about rights and justice is so much phrase mongering; the issue at bottom is one of power, and of power alone.

Now even the apparent approach to reality still betrays willingness to be deluded, for Romain Rolland is just as deluded as ever; the delusion is not one whit less. It could only be so if such people were to discard phrases and recognize that all these things for which they aspire are meaningless as long as they fail to realize that if the old unified state as such—whether a democracy, a republic or a monarchy—does not become threefold, this is simply a way of helping Ahriman's incarnation. Hence all these things, including this recent letter addressed to the world by Romain Rolland, amount to nothing more than rhetorical harangues. People do not grasp the reality, for reality can be grasped only when the necessity for spiritual knowledge and deep penetration into the nature of things is thoroughly understood.

You are all familiar with the much quoted verse: "In the beginning was the Word, and the Word was with God, and the Word was a God." Do people really take these lines in earnest? They utter them, but so often as mere phrases! No particular emphasis is laid on the tense: "In the beginning *was* the Word, and the Word *was* with God, and the Word *was* God." "Word" here must obviously have the meaning it bore in ancient Greece. It is not "word" as understood today—word as mere sound—but it is the inner, spiritual reality. In either case, however, it is the imperfect tense that is employed. The implication therefore is: "In the beginning the Word *was*; but it is no longer." Otherwise the sentence would run: "Now *is* the Word; and the Word is not with God; it *was* with God, and a God *was* the Word but *is* so no longer." This, moreover, is what stands in the Gospel of St. John; otherwise what would be the meaning of the words immediately following: "And the Word was made flesh and dwelt among us." This indicates a further evolution of the Word. "Word" also means anything that human beings can acquire in the way of intellectual wisdom through their efforts and through their intelligence. But it must be quite clear to us that what "word" denotes here is not really the goal for which humanity must strive at the present time or in the immediate future. To express what is now the goal, we should have to say: "Let human beings seek for the Spirit that reveals itself in the Word; for the Spirit *is* with God, and the Spirit *is* a God." Humankind must press on from the word to the spirit, to perception and knowledge of the spirit.

When I remind you of these first verses of the Gospel of St. John, you will realize what little inclination there is today to take such things in earnest and to surmount the arbitrary interpretations so often accepted in matters of the greatest moment. Human intelligence itself must be quickened and illumined by what is revealed in spiritual vision—not that actual seership is essential; what matters is that the fruits of spiritual vision shall be understood. I have repeatedly emphasized that today it is not the seer alone who can apprehend the truth of clairvoyant experience; this apprehension is within the power of everyone at the present time, because the spiritual capacities of human beings are sufficiently mature if they will but resolve to exercise them and are not too indolent to do so. But if the level befitting humanity is to be achieved, such things as were mentioned in the lecture yesterday must be taken in deep earnestness! I used a trivial example to show you how easy it is to be deluded by figures and numbers. Is there not a great deal of superstition where numbers are concerned? What can in some way be *counted* is accepted in science. Natural science loves to weigh, to compute, and social science loves statistics—again a matter of computation and reckoning. It will be difficult indeed for people to bring themselves to admit that all knowledge of the external world acquired through measure and number is so much delusion.

To measure—what does it mean, in reality? It means to compare something with a given dimension, be it length or volume. I can measure a line if I compare it with a line twice, three times, four times, etc., smaller:

In such measurements, no matter whether of lengths or surfaces or weights, the *qualitative* element is entirely lacking. The

number three always remains the same, whether one is count-
ing sheep, human beings, or politicians! It is not a matter of the
qualitative, but only of the quantum, the quantitative. The
essential principle of volume and number is that the qualitative
is left out of account. But for that very reason, all knowledge
derived from the principles of volume and measure is illusion;
and the fact which must be taken in all seriousness is that the
moment we enter the world that can be weighed and measured,
the world of space and time, we enter a world of illusion, a
world that is nothing but a fata morgana as long as we take it to
be reality. It is the ideal of present-day thinking to experience in
connection with all the things of the external world of space
and time, their spatial and temporal significance; whereas, in
truth, what things signify in space and time is their external
aspect only, and we must transcend space and time, penetrating
to much deeper levels, if we are to reach the innermost truth,
the innermost *being* of things. And so a future must come when
people will be able to say: "Yes, with my intelligence I can
apprehend the external world in the way that is the ideal of natural science. But the vista thus presented to me is wholly ahrimanic." This does not mean that natural science is to be ignored
or put aside; it is a matter of realizing that this natural science
leads only to the ahrimanic illusion. Why, then, must people
have natural science, in spite of the fact that it leads only to illusion? It is because in earth existence they are already on the
descending curve of evolution. Of the fourth post-Atlantean
epoch, the Greco-Latin epoch, it may be said that with respect
to knowledge, humanity was, relatively speaking, at the zenith.
But now, in the fifth post-Atlantean epoch, human beings are on
the path of decline, they are a being growing physically weaker,
and to perceive the world in the way the Greeks perceived it
would be too much for their strength.

　　That is something we are not told in history! Just imagine
what modern historians would have to say about it—those
worthy historians who describe Greece as if they were describing some region of their own time because they do not know

that the Greeks looked out into nature with different eyes, listened with different ears from those of modern people. These historians do not tell us that modern human beings would suffer from constant headache or migraine if they were to see and hear in the outer world all that the Greeks saw and heard. The Greeks lived with infinitely greater intensity in the world of the senses. Our own apprehension of this world has already weakened. To be able to bear it, a fata morgana has to be and is presented to us. And not only what we perceive with the senses but on account of our scientific conceptions we "dream" about the external world—that, most emphatically of all, is a fata morgana. The greatest dreamers where the external world is concerned are precisely those who pride themselves on being realistic in their thinking. Darwin and John Stuart Mill are fundamentally dreamers. The dreamers are the very people who claim to be thoroughgoing realists.

But neither must we give ourselves up entirely to our own inner life and impulses. From the way things have developed in the movement represented by the "Theosophical Society," many of you will have realized that cultivation of the inner life alone, as attempted by numbers of people today, does not lead to the goal befitting humanity in the present age. For the all too prevalent tendency is to make no free resolve to transcend ordinary life and attain higher vision but rather to bring into prominence that in us which is not free. All kinds of hallucinatory tendencies, all kinds of faculties fraught with illusion come into play.

It should be realized that just as external science becomes ahrimanic, the higher development of our inner nature becomes luciferic if we give ourselves up to mystical experiences. The luciferic tendency wakens and becomes especially powerful in everyone who, without the self-training described in the book *Knowledge of the Higher Worlds and Its Attainment*, sets about any mystical deepening of the impulses already inherent in their nature. The luciferic tendency shows itself in everyone who begins to brood over experiences of their inner life, and it is extremely powerful in present-day humanity. It takes effect in egoism of which most people are entirely unaware. One comes across so many today who are quite satisfied when they can say of something they have done that they have no cause for self-reproach, that they did it to the best of their knowledge and according to their conscience. That is an entirely luciferic attitude. For in what we do in life the point is not whether or not we have cause to reproach ourselves; what really matters is that we shall take things objectively, with complete detachment, and in accordance with the course of objective facts. And the majority of people today make no effort to achieve this objective understanding or to acquire knowledge of what is necessary for world evolution.

Therefore spiritual science must emphasize the following: That Ahriman is actually preparing for his incarnation; where we can recognize how he is preparing for it; and with what attitude it must be confronted. In such questions the point is not to say: We do this or that in order that we may have no cause for self-reproach—but to learn to recognize the objective facts. We must come to know what is at work in the world, and act accordingly—for the world's sake.

It all amounts to this, that modern people only speak truly of themselves when they say that they hover perpetually between two extremes: between the ahrimanic on the one side, where they are presented with an outer delusion, a fata morgana, and, on the other, the luciferic element within them which induces the tendency to illusions, hallucinations and the like. The ahrimanic tendencies in people today live themselves out in science, the luciferic tendencies, in religion, while in art they swing between the one extreme and the other. In recent times the tendencies of some artists have been more luciferic—they are the expressionists; the tendencies of the others have been more ahrimanic—they are the impressionists. And then, vacillating between all this, there are the people who want to be neither the one nor the other, who do not rightly assess either the luciferic or the ahrimanic but want to avoid both. "Ahriman—no!—*that* I must not, will not do, for it would take me into the realm of the ahrimanic; that I must not, will not do, for it would take me into the realm of the luciferic!" They want to be virtuous, avoiding both the ahrimanic and the luciferic.

But the truth of the matter is that Lucifer and Ahriman must be regarded as two scales of a balance and it is we who must hold the beam in equipoise.

And how can we train ourselves to do this? By permeating what takes ahrimanic form within us with a strongly luciferic element. What is it that arises in modern people in an Ahrimanic form? It is his knowledge of the outer world. There is nothing more ahrimanic than this knowledge of the material world, for it is sheer illusion. Nevertheless if the fata morgana that arises out of chemistry, out of physics, out of astronomy and the like can fill us with fiery enthusiasm and interest, then through our interest—which is itself luciferic—we can wrest from Ahriman what is his own.

That, however, is just what human beings have no desire to do; they find it irksome. And many people who flee from external, materialistic knowledge are misconceiving their task and preparing the best possible incarnation for Ahriman in earth existence. Again, what wells up in our inmost being today is very strongly luciferic. How can we train ourselves rightly in this direction? By diving into it with our ahrimanic nature, that is to say, by trying to avoid all illusions about our own inner life and impulses and observing *ourselves* just as we observe the outer world. Modern people must realize how urgent it is to educate themselves in this way. Anyone who has an observant eye in these matters will often come across circumstances of which the following is an example.

A man tells someone how indignant he is with countless human beings. He describes minutely how this or that in *a*, in *b*, in *c*, and so on, angers him. He has not an inkling that he is simply talking about his own characteristics. This peculiarity in human beings was never so widespread as it is today. And those who believe they are free of it, are the greatest culprits. The essential is that people should approach their own inner nature with ahrimanic cold-bloodedness and dispassion. Their inner nature is still fiery enough even when cooled down in this way! There is no need to fear that it will be over-cooled.

If the right stand is to be taken to Ahriman's future incarnation, people must become more objective where their own impulses are concerned, and far, far more subjective where the external world is concerned—not by introducing pictures of fantasy but by bringing interest, alert attention, and devotion to the things of immediate life.

When people find one thing or another in outer life tedious, possibly because of the education they have received or because of other circumstances, the path which Ahriman wants to take for the benefit of his incarnation is greatly smoothed. Tedium is so widespread nowadays! I have known numbers of people who find it irksome to acquaint themselves for example with banking procedure, or the stock exchange, or single or double entry bookkeeping. But that is never the right attitude. It simply means that the point has not been discovered where a thing burns with interest. Once this point is reached, even a dry cashbook can become just as interesting as Schiller's *Maid of Orleans*, or Shakespeare's *Hamlet*, or anything else—even Raphael's *Sistine Madonna*. It is only a question of finding the point at which every single thing in life becomes interesting.

What I have just said may make you think that all these matters are very paradoxical. But in reality they are not. It is we who are paradoxical in our relationship to truth. What we must realize—and this is a dire necessity today—is that *we*, not the world, are at fault. Nothing does more to prepare the path for Ahriman's incarnation than to find this or that tedious, to consider oneself superior to one thing or another and refuse to enter into it. Again it is the same question of finding the point where everything is of interest. It is never a matter of a subjective rejection or acceptance of things, but of an objective recognition of the extent to which things are either luciferic or ahrimanic, with the result that the scales are overweighted on the one side or the other.

To be interested in something does not mean that one considers it justifiable. It means simply that one develops an inner energy to get to grips with it and steer it into the right channel.

As some of you may know—it is a long time ago now—a number of friends bought themselves books on mathematics. A kind of "sporting spirit" had crept into them! They bought the works of Lubsen[1] but it was not long before most of the volumes found their way to library shelves and the mathematical knowledge was not much in evidence! This, of course, is not meant as a hint to tackle the matter again—I am making no such suggestion. But to come to grips with something in which, to begin with, one is not interested at all, in order that a new understanding of world existence may arise—that is of untold significance. For such things as I want to bring home to you in these lectures—how Lucifer and Ahriman intervene in the evolution of humankind side by side with the Christ impulse— these things must be taken in all earnestness and their consequences rightly assessed.

Had there been no luciferic wisdom, no understanding of the Mystery of Golgotha could have been acquired through the gnosis in the early centuries of Christendom. Understanding of the Mystery of Golgotha diminished with the fading of the luciferic wisdom. And where is there any evidence today of such understanding? The fact that understanding cannot be found through external, ahrimanic science is perceived by those who to some extent recognize its characteristics. Take, for example, a man like Cardinal Newman—a very significant figure in the sphere of religion during the second half of the nineteenth century. At his investiture as Cardinal in Rome, he declared that he could see no salvation for the religious devel-

---

1. Heinrich Borchert Lubsen (1801-64).

opment of humankind other than a new revelation![1] But there
it remained. He himself showed no special inclination to
receive anything of the new spiritual life that can now stream
into humanity out of the spiritual worlds. What he said
remained in the sphere of abstraction.

In very truth humanity needs a new revelation. Of this
there is evidence on all sides. There have been discussions
recently about the deterioration in morals and in the general
attitude toward morality during the last four or five years. The
conclusion reached is that denominational religious instruction
must be introduced more intensively into the schools. But it
cannot be emphasized often enough that this instruction was
already being given and the times are supposed to have come
under its influence. If the old denominational instruction is
again to be introduced we shall simply be beginning the whole
process over again. In a short time we shall be back where we
were in 1914. It is in the highest degree important to realize that
in the subconsciousness of human beings there are longings
quite different in character from what comes to expression on
the surface.

When we founded the Waldorf School in Stuttgart earlier
this year, we were obliged to arrange for the religious instruction to be divided among the various clergy. A particular hour
is devoted to religious instruction, which is given by a Catholic
priest for the Catholic children and by an Evangelical pastor for
the Evangelicals. I shall not speak of the difficulties that came
from the side of the priests—that is a chapter by itself. What I
do want to say, however, is that an immediate desire was
expressed for religious teaching apart from any denomination.

1. See his speech in Rome, May 12, 1879, when he had been raised to the rank of Cardinal. "...Hitherto the civil power has been Christian. Even in countries separated from
the Church, as in my own, the *dictum* was in force, when I was young, that 'Christianity
was the law of the land.' Now, everywhere that goodly framework of society, which is
the creation of Christianity, is throwing off Christianity. The *dictum* to which I have
referred, with a hundred others which followed upon it, is gone, or is going everywhere; and by the end of the century, unless the Almighty interferes, it will be forgotten." (*The Life of John Henry Newman*, by Wilfrid Ward, Vol. 2, p. 460.)

At first I thought that the attendance would be insignificant in comparison with the numbers attending the denominational instruction. But in spite of the fact that soon there will not be a single pulpit in Stuttgart from which invectives are not poured on Anthroposophy, a large number of children—five times as many as we expected—have asked for a kind of anthroposophical instruction in religion, and the class has had to be divided into two. Subjectively this may not be altogether welcome, for it may prove to be a rod for our own backs. But of that I do not want to speak. I want only to show that there *is* a longing for progress in human beings but that they are asleep and do not perceive that forces are keeping these longings in subjection. And moreover the courage to bring these longings to the surface is very largely lacking.

Just think what the effect could be of knowledge such as that of the future incarnation of Ahriman, who is preparing for it by means I have been describing both yesterday and today. It is essential to inform ourselves objectively about these things in order that we may take the right stand toward what is going on around us in the way of preparation for the Ahriman incarnation. Only if you apply deep and mature reflection to what has been said in these lectures about the ahrimanic currents will you be able to apprehend the gravity of the present situation.

LECTURE THREE

THE PHASE OF EVOLUTION beginning in our own time has a very special character. The same may, of course, be said of each epoch but in every case it is a matter of defining the particular characteristics. The present phase of evolution may be characterized in a general way by saying that all the experiences confronting humankind in the *physical* world during the earth's further existence will represent a decline, a retrogression. The time when human progress was made possible through the constant refinement of the physical forces is already over. In the future, too, humankind will progress, but only through *spiritual* development, through development on a higher level than that of the processes of the physical plane. People who rely entirely on the processes of the physical plane will find in them no source of satisfaction. An indication given in spiritual science a long time ago, in the lecture course on the Apocalypse,[1] namely that we are heading for the "War of All against All," must from now onward be grasped in all its significance and gravity; its implications must not remain in the realm of theory but also come to expression in the actions, the whole behavior of human beings.

The fact that—to use a colloquialism—people in the future are not going to get much fun out of developments on the

1. Twelve lectures given at Nürnberg, 1908.

physical plane will bring home to them that further evolution must proceed from *spiritual* forces.

This can be understood only by surveying a lengthy period of evolution and applying what is discovered to experiences that will become more and more general in the future. The trend of forces that will manifest in the well-nigh rhythmical onset of war and destruction—processes of which the present catastrophe is but the beginning—will become only too evident. It is childish to believe that anything connected with this war can bring about a permanent era of peace for humanity on the physical plane. That will not be so. What must come about on the earth is *spiritual development*. Its direction and purport will be clear to us if, after surveying a comparatively lengthy epoch preceding the Mystery of Golgotha, we bear in mind something of the meaning of the Mystery of Golgotha and then try to envisage the impulse of that event working in the future evolution of humankind.

We have studied the Mystery of Golgotha from many different points of view and will do so again today by characterizing, very briefly, the civilization which preceded it—let us say as far back as the third millennium B.C.—and then continued for a time as pagan culture in the period of Christian development itself. Within this pagan culture, the utterly different Hebraic-Jewish culture took root, having Christianity as its offspring.

The nature of pagan culture can best be understood if we realize that it was the outcome of knowledge, vision and action born of forces much wider in range than those belonging to present earthly existence. It was actually through Hebraic culture that the *moral element* was first inculcated into humanity. In paganism the moral element did not occupy a place separate and apart; this pagan culture was such that people felt themselves members of the whole cosmos.

This is something we must particularly bear in mind. Human beings living on earth within the old pagan world felt themselves membered into the whole cosmos. They felt how the forces at work in the movements of the stars extend into their own action, or, better said, into the forces taking effect in their actions. What later passed for astrology, and does so still, is but a reflection—and a very misleading one at that—of the ancient wisdom gleaned from contemplation of the stars in their courses and then used as the basis for precepts governing human action.

These ancient civilizations can be understood only if light is thrown by spiritual science upon human evolution in its outer aspect some four or five thousand years before Christ.

We are apt to speak in rather a matter-of-fact way of the second or the first post-Atlantean epochs, but we err if we picture human existence on the earth in the fifth, sixth, or seventh millennia B.C. as having been similar to our present existence. It is quite correct that people living on the earth in those ancient times had a kind of instinctive soul life, in a certain respect more akin to the soul life of animals than to that of present-day human beings. But it is a very one-sided conception of human life to say that in those ancient times people were more like animals. In tenor of soul, the human being then moving about the earth was, it is true, more like the animal; but those human-animal bodies were used by beings of soul and spirit who felt themselves members of the supersensible worlds, above all of the cosmic worlds. And provided we go back far enough, say to the fifth pre-Christian millennium, it may be said that people made use of animal bodies as instruments rather than feeling themselves within those bodies. To characterize these people accurately, one would have to say that when they were awake, they moved about with an instinctive life of soul like that of animals, but into this instinctive life of soul there shone something like dreams from their sleeping state, waking dreams. And in these waking dreams they perceived how they had descended, to use animal bodies merely as instruments. This inner, fundamental tenor of the human soul then came to expression as a religious rite, in the Mithras cult with its main symbol of the God Mithras riding on a bull, above him the starry heavens to which *he* belongs, and below him the earth to which the bull belongs. This symbol was not, strictly speaking, a symbol to these people of old; it was a vision of *reality*. People's whole tenor of soul made them say to themselves: When I am outside my body at night I belong to the forces of the cosmos, of the starry heavens; when I wake in the morning I make use of animal instincts in an animal body.

Then human evolution passed, figuratively speaking, into a period of twilight. A certain dimness, a certain lethargy, spread over the life of humanity; the cosmic dreams receded and instinct gained the upper hand.

The attitude of soul formerly prevailing in human beings was preserved through the Mysteries, mainly through the Asiatic Mysteries. But in the fourth millennium B.C. and until the beginning of the third, humanity in general—when uninfluenced by the Mystery wisdom—lived an existence pervaded by a more or less dim, twilight consciousness. In Asia and the then-known world, it may be said that during the fourth and at the beginning of the third millennium before the Mystery of Golgotha, people's life of soul was dim and instinctive. But the Mysteries were there, into which, through the powerful rites and ceremonies, the spiritual worlds were able to penetrate. And it was from these centers that human beings received illumination.

At the beginning of the third millennium a momentous event took place. The root cause of this dim, more instinctive life may be characterized by saying that as beings of spirit and soul, people were still unable at that time to make use of the human organs of intellect. These organs were already within them, they had taken shape in their physical constitution, but the being of spirit and soul could not make use of them. Thus human beings could not acquire knowledge through their own thinking, through their own powers of intellectual discernment. They were dependent upon what was imparted to them from the Mysteries. And then, about the beginning of the third millennium, a momentous event took place in the east of Asia.

A child of a distinguished Asiatic family of the time was allowed to grow up in the precincts of the Mystery ceremonies. Circumstances were such that this child was actually permitted to take part in the ceremonies, undoubtedly because the priests conducting the rites in the Mysteries felt it as an inspiration that such a child must be allowed to participate. And when the being incarnate in that child had reached the age of about forty—approximately that age—something very remarkable came to light. It became evident—and there is no doubt at all that the priests of the Mysteries had foreseen the event prophetically—it became evident that this man who had been allowed to grow up in the precincts of one of the Mystery centers in East Asia, began suddenly, at the age of about forty, to grasp through the faculty of human intellect itself what had formerly come into the Mysteries through revelation, and only through revelation. He was as it were the first to make use of the organs of human intellect, but still in association with the Mysteries.

Translating into terms of our present language how the priests of the Mysteries spoke of this matter, we must say: In this man, Lucifer himself was incarnated—no more and no less than that! It is a significant, momentous fact that in the third millennium before Christ an incarnation of Lucifer in the flesh actually took place in the east of Asia. And from this incarnation of Lucifer in the flesh—for this being became a teacher—there went forth what is described as the pre-Christian, pagan culture which still survived in the gnosis of the earliest Christian centuries.

It would be wrong to pass derogatory judgment on this Lucifer culture. For all the beauty produced by Greek civilization, even the insight that is still alive in ancient Greek philosophy and in the tragedies of Aeschylus would have been impossible without this Lucifer incarnation.

The influence of the Lucifer incarnation was still powerful in the south of Europe, in the north of Africa, and in Asia Minor during the first centuries of Christendom. And when the Mystery of Golgotha had taken place on earth, it was essentially the luciferic wisdom through which it could be understood. The gnosis, which set about the task of grasping the import of the Mystery of Golgotha, was impregnated through and through with luciferic wisdom. It must therefore be emphasized, firstly, that at the beginning of the third millennium B.C. there was a Chinese incarnation of Lucifer; at the beginning of our own era the incarnation of Christ took place. And to begin with, the significance of the incarnation of Christ was grasped because the power of the old Lucifer incarnation still survived. This power did not actually fade from the human faculty of comprehension until the fourth century A.D.; and even then, it had its aftermath, its ramifications.

To these two incarnations, the Lucifer incarnation in ancient times and the incarnation of the Christ which gives the earth its meaning, a third incarnation will be added in a future not so very far distant. And the events of the present time are already moving in such a way as to prepare for it.

Of the incarnation of Lucifer at the beginning of the third millennium B.C., we must say: through Lucifer, human beings have acquired the faculty of using the organs of their intellect, of their power of intellectual discernment. It was Lucifer himself, in a human body, who was the first to grasp through the power of intellect what formerly could be imparted to humanity only through revelation, namely, the content of the Mysteries.

What is now in preparation and will quite definitely come to pass on earth in a none-too-distant future is an actual incarnation of Ahriman.

As you know, since the middle of the fifteenth century we have been living in an era in which it behooves humankind to come more and more into possession of the full power of *consciousness*. It is of the very greatest importance that people should approach the coming incarnation of Ahriman with full consciousness of this event. The incarnation of Lucifer could be recognized only by the prophetic insight of the priests of the

Mysteries. People were also very unconscious of what the incarnation of Christ and the event of Golgotha really signified. But they must live on toward the incarnation of Ahriman with full consciousness amid the shattering events which will occur on the physical plane. Amid the perpetual stresses of war and other tribulations of the immediate future, the human mind will become very inventive in the domain of physical life. And through this very growth of inventiveness in physical life— which cannot be averted in any way or by any means—the bodily existence of a human individuality in whom Ahriman can incarnate will become possible and inevitable.

From the spiritual world this Ahrimanic power is preparing for incarnation on the earth, endeavoring in every conceivable way to make such preparation that the incarnation of Ahriman in human form may be able to mislead and corrupt humankind on earth to the uttermost. A task of humankind during the next phase of civilization will be to live toward the incarnation of Ahriman with such alert consciousness that this incarnation can actually serve to promote a higher, spiritual development, inasmuch as through Ahriman himself humanity will become aware of what can, or shall we say, can *not* be achieved by physical life alone. But people must go forward with full consciousness toward this incarnation of Ahriman and become more and more alert in every domain, in order to recognize with greater and greater clarity those trends in life which are leading toward this Ahrimanic incarnation. People must learn from spiritual science to find the key to life and so be able to recognize and learn to control the currents leading toward the incarnation of Ahriman. It must be realized that Ahriman will live among people on the earth, but that in confronting him people will themselves determine what they may learn from him, what they may receive from him. This, however, they will not be able to do unless, from now onward, they take control of certain spiritual and also unspiritual currents which otherwise are used by Ahriman for the purpose of leaving humankind as deeply unconscious as possible of his coming; then, one day, he will be able to appear on earth and overwhelm people tempting and luring them to repudiate earth evolution, thus preventing it from reaching its goal. To understand the whole process of which I have been speaking, it is essential to recognize the character of certain currents and influences—spiritual or the reverse.

Do you not see the continually growing number of people at the present time who do not want any science of the spirit, any knowledge of the spiritual? Do you not see how numerous are the people to whom the old forces of religion no longer give any inner stimulus? Whether they go to church or not is a matter of complete indifference to large numbers of human beings nowadays. The old religious impulses mean nothing to them. But neither will they bring themselves to give a thought to what can stream into our civilization as new spiritual life. They resist it, reject it, regard it as folly, as something inconvenient; they will not allow themselves to have anything to do with it. But, you see, human beings as we live on earth are veritably a unity. Our spiritual nature cannot be separated from our physical nature; both work together as a unity between birth and death. And even if human beings do not receive the spiritual through their faculties of soul, the spiritual takes effect, nevertheless. Since the last third of the nineteenth century the spiritual has been streaming around us; it is streaming into earthly evolution. The spiritual is there in very truth—only people are not willing to receive it.

But even if they do not accept the spiritual, it *is there*! And what becomes of it? Paradoxical as it may seem—for much that is true seems paradoxical to the modern mind—in those people who refuse the spiritual and like eating and drinking best of all things in life, the spiritual streams, unconsciously to them, into the processes of eating and digestion. This is the secret of that march into materialism which began about the year 1840, or rather was then in active preparation. Those who do not receive the spiritual through their souls receive it today nonetheless: in eating and drinking they eat and drink the spirit.

They are "eaters" of the soul and spirit. And in this way the spirit that is streaming into earth evolution passes over into the luciferic element, is conveyed to Lucifer. Thereby the luciferic power, which can then be of help to the ahrimanic power for its later incarnation, is constantly strengthened. This must come to the knowledge of those who admit the fact that in the future people will either receive spiritual knowledge consciously or consume the spirit unconsciously, thereby delivering it into the hands of the luciferic powers.

This stream of spirit-and-soul-consumption is particularly encouraged by Ahriman because in this way he can lull humankind into greater and greater drowsiness, so that then, through his incarnation, he will be able to come among people and fall upon them unawares because they do not confront him consciously.

But Ahriman can also make direct preparation for his incarnation, and he does so. Certainly, people of our day also have a spiritual life, but it is purely intellectual, unconnected with the spiritual world. This purely intellectual life is becoming more and more widespread; at first it took effect mainly in the sciences, but now it is leading to mischiefs of every kind in social life as well. What is the essential character of this intellectual life?

This intellectual life has very little to do with the true interests of human beings! I ask you: how many teachers do you not see today, passing in and out of higher and lower educational institutions without bringing any inner enthusiasm to their science but pursuing it merely as a means of livelihood? In such cases the interest of the soul is not directly linked with the actual pursuit. The same thing happens even at school. Think how much is learned at the various stages of life without any real enthusiasm or interest, how external the intellectual life is becoming for many people who devote themselves to it! And how many there are today who are forced to produce a mass of intellectual material which is then preserved in libraries and, as spiritual life, is not truly alive!

Everything that is developing as intellectual life without being suffused by warmth of soul, without being quickened by enthusiasm, directly furthers the incarnation of Ahriman in a way that is after his own heart. It lulls people to sleep in the way I have described, so that its results are advantageous to Ahriman.

There are numerous other currents in the spiritual or unspiritual life which Ahriman can turn to his advantage. You have lately heard—and you are still hearing it—that national states, national empires must be founded. A great deal is said about "freedom of the individual peoples." But the time for founding empires based on relationships of blood and race is past and over in the evolution of mankind. If an appeal is made today to national, racial, and similar relationships, to relationships arising out of the intellect and not out of the spirit, then disharmony among humankind will be intensified. And it is this disharmony among humankind which the ahrimanic power can put to special use. Chauvinism, perverted patriotism in every form—this is the material from which Ahriman will build just what he needs.

But there are other things as well. Everywhere today we see parties being formed for one object or another. People nowadays have no discernment, nor do they desire to have it where party opinions and party programs are concerned. With intellectual ingenuity, proof can be furnished in support of the most radically opposing theories. Very clever arguments can be used to prove the soundness of Leninism—but the same applies to directly contrary principles and also to what lies between the two extremes. An excellent case can be made out for every party program: but the one who establishes the validity of the opposite program is equally right. The intellectualism prevailing among people today is not capable of demonstrating the *inner* potentialities and values of anything. It can furnish proofs; but what is intellectually proved should not be regarded as of real value or efficacy in life. People oppose one another in parties because the soundness of every party opinion—at any rate the main party opinions—can be proved with equal justification. Our intellect remains at the surface layer of understanding and does not penetrate to the deeper layer where the truth actually lies. This, too, must be fundamentally and thoroughly understood.

People today prefer to let their intellect remain on the surface and not to penetrate with deeper forces to those levels where the essential nature of things is disclosed. It is only necessary to look around a little, for even where it takes its most external form, life often reveals the pitfalls of current predilections. People love numbers and figures in science, but they also love figures in the social sphere as well. Social science consists almost entirely of statistics. And from statistics, that is to say from figures, the weightiest conclusions are reached. Well, with figures too, anything can be proved and anything believed; for figures are not a means whereby the essential reality of things can be proved—they are simply a means of deception! Whenever one fails to look beyond figures to the *qualitative*, they can be utterly deceptive.

The following is an obvious example. There is, or at least there used to be, a great deal of argument about the nationality of the Macedonians. In the political life of the Balkan peninsula, much depended upon the statistics compiled there. The figures are of just as much value as those contained in other statistics. Whether statistics are compiled of wheat and rye production, or of the numbers of Greek, Serbian, or Bulgarian nationals in Macedonia—in regard to what can be *proved* by these means it is all the same. From the figures quoted for the Greeks, for the Bulgarians, for the Serbians, very plausible conclusions can be drawn. But one can also have an eye for the qualitative element, and then one often finds it recorded that the father was Greek, one son was Bulgarian, another was Serbian. What is at the back of it you can puzzle out for yourselves! These statistics are taken as authoritative, whereas in this case they were compiled solely in support of party aims. It stands to reason that if the father is really a Greek, the two sons are also Greeks. But the procedure adopted there is just an example of many other things that are done with figures. Ahriman can achieve a great deal through figures and numbers used in this way as evidence of proof.

A further means of which Ahriman can avail himself is again one that will seem paradoxical. As you know, we have been concerned in our movement to study the Gospels in the light of spiritual science. But these deeper interpretations of the Gospels, which are becoming more and more necessary in our time, are rejected on all sides, just as spiritual science as a whole is rejected.

The people who often profess humility in these matters— and they are insistent about it—are actually the most arrogant of all. More and more generally it is being said that people should steep themselves in the very simplicity of the Gospels and not attempt to understand the Mystery of Golgotha by entering into the complexities of spiritual science. Those who feign unpretentiousness in their study of the Gospels are the most arrogant of all, for they despise the honest search for knowledge demanded in spiritual science. So arrogant are they that they believe the highest revelations of the spiritual world can be garnered without effort, simply by browsing on the simplicity of the Gospels. What claims to be "humble" or "simple" today is often supreme arrogance. In sects, in religious confessions—it is there that the most arrogant people are to be found.

It must be remembered that the Gospels came into existence at a time when the luciferic wisdom still survived. In the first centuries of Christendom, people's understanding of the Gospels was quite different from what it came to be in later times. Today, people who cannot deepen their minds through spiritual science merely pretend to understand the Gospels. In reality they have no idea even of the original meaning of the words; for the translations that have been made into the different languages are not faithful reproductions of the Gospels; often they are scarcely even reminiscent of the original meaning of the words in which the Gospels were composed.

Real understanding of the intervention of the Christ being in earthly evolution is possible today only through spiritual science. Those who want to study, or actually do study the Gospels "without pretension"—as the saying goes—cannot come to any inner realization of the Christ being as he truly is, but only to an illusory picture, or, at very most, a vision or hallucination of the Christ being. No real connection with the Christ impulse can be achieved today merely through reading the Gospels—but only a hallucinatory picture of the Christ. Hence the prevalence of the theological view that the Christ was not present in the man Jesus of Nazareth, who was simply an historical figure like Socrates or Plato or others, although possibly more exalted. The "simple man of Nazareth" is an ideal even to the theologians. And very few of them indeed can make anything of an event like Paul's vision at the gate of Damascus, because without the deepened knowledge yielded by spiritual science the Gospels can give rise only to a hallucination of the Christ, not to vision of the real Christ. And so Paul's vision at Damascus is also regarded as an hallucination.

Deeper understanding of the Gospels in the light of spiritual science is essential today, for the apathy that takes hold of people who are content to live merely within the arms of the denominations will be used to the utmost by Ahriman in order to achieve his goal—which is that his incarnation shall catch people unawares. And those who believe they are being most truly Christian by rejecting any development of the conception of the Christ mystery, are, in their arrogance, the ones who do most to promote Ahriman's aims. The denominations and sects are positively spheres of encouragement, breeding-grounds for Ahriman. It is futile to gloss these things over with illusions. Just as the materialistic attitude, rejecting the spiritual altogether and contending that the human being is a product of what people eat and drink, furthers Ahriman's aims, so are these aims furthered by the stubborn rejection of everything spiritual and adherence to the literal, "simple" conception of the Gospels.

You see, a barrier which prevents the single Gospels from unduly circumscribing the human mind has been erected through the fact that the event of Golgotha is described in the Gospels from four—seemingly contradictory—sides. Only a little reflection will show that this is a protection from too literal a conception. In sects, however, where *one* Gospel only is taken as the basis of the teaching—and such sects are quite numerous—pitfalls, stupefaction, and hallucination are generated. In their day, the Gospels were given as a necessary counterweight to the luciferic gnosis; but if no attempt is made to develop understanding of their content, the aims of Ahriman are furthered, not the progress of humankind. In the absolute sense, nothing is good in itself, but is always good or bad according to the use to which it is put. The best can be the worst if wrongly used. Sublime though they are, the Gospels can also have the opposite effect if people are too lazy to search for a deeper understanding based on spiritual science.

Hence there is a great deal in the spiritual and unspiritual currents of the present time of which people should be acutely aware, and determine their attitude of soul accordingly. Upon the ability and willingness to penetrate to the roots of such matters will depend the effect which the incarnation of Ahriman can have upon human beings, whether this incarnation will lead them to prevent the earth from reaching its goal, or bring home to them the very limited significance of intellectual, unspiritual life. If people rightly take in hand the currents leading toward Ahriman, then simply through his incarnation in earthly life they will recognize the ahrimanic influence on the one side, and on the other its polar opposite—the luciferic influence. And then the very contrast between the ahrimanic and the luciferic will enable them to perceive the third reality. Human beings must consciously wrestle through to an understanding of this trinity of the Christian impulse, the ahrimanic and the luciferic influences; for without this consciousness they will not be able to go forward into the future with the prospect of achieving the goal of earth existence.

Spiritual science must be taken in deep earnestness, for only so can it be rightly understood. It is not the outcome of any sectarian whim but something that has proceeded from the fundamental needs of human evolution. Those who recognize these needs cannot choose between whether they will or will not endeavor to foster spiritual science. On the contrary they will say to themselves: The whole physical and spiritual life of human beings must be illumined and pervaded by the conceptions of spiritual science!

Just as once in the East there was a Lucifer incarnation, and then, at the midpoint, as it were, of world evolution, the incarnation of Christ, so in the West there will be an incarnation of Ahriman.

This ahrimanic incarnation cannot be averted; it is inevitable, for humanity must confront Ahriman face to face. He will be the individuality by whom it will be made clear what indescribable cleverness can be developed if they call to their help all that earthly forces can do to enhance cleverness and ingenuity. In the catastrophes that will befall humanity in the near future, people will become extremely inventive; many things discovered in the forces and substances of the universe will be used to provide human nourishment. But these very discoveries will at the same time make it apparent that matter is connected with the organs of intellect, not with the organs of the spirit but of the intellect. People will learn what to eat and drink in order to become really clever. Eating and drinking cannot make them spiritual, but clever and astute, yes. Humanity has no knowledge of these things as yet; but not only will they be striven for, they will be the inevitable outcome of catastrophes looming in the near future. And certain secret societies—where preparations are already in train—will apply these things in such a way that the necessary conditions can be established for an actual incarnation of Ahriman on the earth. This incarnation cannot be averted, for people must realize during the time of the earth's existence just how much can proceed from purely material processes! We must learn to bring under our control those spiritual or unspiritual currents which are leading to Ahriman.

Once it is realized that conflicting party programs can be proved equally correct, our attitude of soul will be that we do not set out to *prove* things, but rather to *experience* them. For to experience a thing is a very different matter from attempting to prove it intellectually.

Equally we shall be convinced that deeper and deeper penetration of the Gospels is necessary through spiritual science. The literal, word-for-word acceptance of the Gospels that is still so prevalent today promotes ahrimanic culture. Even on external grounds it is obvious that a strictly literal acceptance of the Gospels is unjustified. For as you know, what is good and right for *one* time is not right for every other time. What is right for one epoch becomes luciferic or ahrimanic when practiced in a later one. The mere reading of the Gospel texts has had its day. What is essential now is to acquire a *spiritual* understanding of the Mystery of Golgotha in the light of the truths enshrined in the Gospels. Many people, of course, find these things disquieting; but those whose interest is attracted by anthroposophy must learn to realize that the levels of culture, gradually piling one above the other, have created chaos, and that light must penetrate again into this chaos.

It is interesting nowadays to listen to someone whose views have become very extreme, or to read about some burning question of the day, and then to listen to sermons on the same subject given by a priest of some denomination who is still steeped in the form of thought current in bygone times. There you face two worlds which you cannot possibly confuse unless you avoid all attempts to get at the root of these things. Listen to a modern socialist speaking about social questions and then, immediately afterward, to a Catholic preacher speaking about the same questions. It is very interesting to find two levels of culture existing side by side but using the words in an entirely different sense. The same word has quite a different meaning in each case.

These things should be seen in the light that will dawn if they are taken in the earnest spirit we have been trying to convey. People belonging to definite religions do also come, in the end, to long in their way for spiritual deepening. It is by no means without significance that a man as eminently spiritual as Cardinal Newman, ardent Catholic though he was, should say at his investiture in Rome that he could see no salvation for Christianity other than a new revelation.

In effect, what Cardinal Newman said was that he could see no salvation for Christianity other than a new revelation! But he had not the courage to take a new *spiritual* revelation seriously. And so it is with many others. You can read countless treatises today about what is needed in social life. Another book has recently appeared: *Socialism*, by Robert Wilbrandt, the son of the poet. In it the social question is discussed on the foundation of accurate and detailed knowledge. And finally it is stated that without the spirit nothing is achieved, that the very course of events shows that the spirit is necessary. Yes, but what does such a man really achieve? He gets as far as to utter the word "spirit," to *pronounce* the abstract word "spirit"; but he refuses to accept, indeed he rejects, anything that endeavors to make the spirit really take effect.

For that, it is essential above all to realize that wallowing in abstractions, however loud the cry for the spirit, is not yet spiritual, not yet spirit! Vague, abstract chattering about the spirit must never be confused with the active search for the content of the spiritual world pursued in anthroposophical science.

Nowadays there is much talk about the spirit. But you who accept spiritual science should not be deluded by such chattering; you should perceive the difference between it and the descriptions of the spiritual world attempted in anthroposophy, where the spiritual world is described as objectively as the physical world. You should probe into these differences, reminding yourselves repeatedly that abstract talk of the spirit is a deviation from sincere striving for the spirit and that, by their very talk, people are actually removing themselves from the spirit. Purely intellectual allusion to the spirit leads nowhere. What, then, is "intelligence"? What is the content of our human intelligence? I can best explain this in the following way. Imagine—and this will be better understood by the many ladies present!—imagine yourself standing in front of a mirror and looking into it. The picture presented to you by the mirror is *you*, but it has no reality at all. It is nothing but a reflection. All the intelligence within your soul, all the intellectual content, is only a mirror image; it has no reality. And just as your reflected image is called into existence through the mirror, so what mirrors itself as intelligence is called into existence through the physical apparatus of your body, through the brain. You are intelligent only because your body is there. And as little as you can touch yourself by stretching your hand toward your reflected image, as little can you lay hold of the spirit if you turn only to the intellectual—for the spirit is not there! What is grasped through the intellect, ingenious as it may be, never contains the spirit itself, but only a picture of the spirit. You cannot truly experience the spirit if you get no further than mere intelligence. The reason why intelligence is so seductive is that it yields a picture, a reflected picture of the spirit—but not the spirit itself. It seems unnecessary to go to the inconvenience of penetrating to the spirit, because it is there—or so, at least, one imagines. In reality it is only a reflected picture—but for all that, it is not difficult to talk about the spirit.

To distinguish the mere picture from the reality—that is the task of the tenor of soul which does not merely theorize about spiritual science but has actual perception of the spirit.

That is what I wanted to say to you today in order to intensify the earnestness which should pervade our whole attitude to the spiritual life as conceived by anthroposophy. For the evolution of humanity in the future will depend upon how truly this attitude is adopted by people of the present day. If what I have characterized in this lecture continues to be offered the reception that is still offered to it today by the vast majority of people on the earth, then Ahriman will be an evil guest when he comes. But if people are able to rouse themselves to take into their consciousness what we have been studying, if they are able so to guide it that humanity can freely confront the ahrimanic influence, then, when Ahriman appears, human beings will acquire, precisely through him, the power to realize that although the earth must enter inevitably into its decline, humankind is lifted above earthly existence through this very fact. When human beings have reached a certain age in physical life, the body begins to decline, but if they are sensible they make no complaint, knowing that together with the soul they are approaching a life that does not run parallel with this physical decline. There lives in humankind something that is not bound up with the already prevailing decline of the physical earth but becomes more and more spiritual just because of this physical decline.

Let us learn to say frankly: Yes, the earth is in its decline, and human life, too, with respect to its physical manifestation; but just because it is so, let us muster the strength to draw into our civilization that element which, springing from humankind itself, will live on while the earth is in decline, as the immortal fruit of earth evolution.

LECTURE FOUR

WE HAVE HEARD THAT THE human soul was once endowed with a kind of primeval wisdom, that this wisdom gradually faded away and is now no longer accessible. Consequently with respect to their knowledge, people feel thrown back more and more upon what is presented to them by physical existence. By "knowledge" I do not mean only science in the accepted sense, but the knowledge that is consciously applied by the soul in the ordinary affairs of life.

The question will naturally arise: how did this ancient wisdom actually come into being? Here I must touch upon a new aspect of matters we have often considered from other angles.

Let us look back to the time when human beings began in the real sense to be citizens of the earth, when as beings of soul and spirit they came down to the earth, surrounded themselves with its forces and became earthly beings. If human beings had simply descended to the earth with the qualities inherent in their own nature, evolution would have taken quite a different course through the various epochs of culture. But having made the descent, human beings would have been obliged to establish a relationship with the surrounding world, to acquire earthly knowledge—I will not say through clairvoyance in the proper sense—but through instincts imbued with a certain measure of clairvoyance. The acquisition of this earthly knowledge would have been a very slow and gradual process and for long ages people would have remained ineffectual, childish beings. By our own time they would, it is true, have succeeded in developing a constitution of soul and body compatible with humanness, but they would never have reached the spiritual heights they have actually attained. That they were able to achieve this evolution in a way other than by passing through all the stages of childhood is due to the intervention in earthly evolution of the luciferic beings. We know from recent lectures that the Lucifer individuality himself incarnated in Asia in a certain epoch of pre-Christian times, and that the original pagan wisdom to which many historical data bear witness proceeded from this being. But the luciferic beings have from the very beginning been associated in some way with the evolution of humanity.

I beg you earnestly—although I know that such requests are of little avail—not to adopt a philistine attitude when mention is made of luciferic beings. Even among anthroposophists there is still the tendency to say: "That is certainly luciferic. At all costs let us avoid it, reject it!" But these things have to be considered in many different aspects and it must always be remembered that the whole of the old pagan wisdom emanated from a luciferic source. The subject is one that calls for deep and serious study.

The farther back we go in the evolution of humanity, the more do we find certain individuals who through the qualities attained in earlier incarnations were sufficiently mature to apprehend the treasures of wisdom possessed by the luciferic beings. Think, for example, of the seven Holy Rishis of ancient India. When Indians interpreted the wisdom of the Holy Rishis, they knew, if they had been initiated into these things, that the teachers of the Rishis were luciferic beings. For what the luciferic beings brought with them into earth evolution was, above all, the world of thought, of intellectualistic thought pervading culture, the world of reason in the highest sense of the word—the world of wisdom. And going back to the primeval origins of human existence, we find that the sources of pagan wisdom always lie with luciferic beings.

It may be asked: How is this possible? We must realize that human beings would have remained children had they not received from the Mysteries the constant instruction that emanated from luciferic beings. Those who possessed the knowledge and the inherited, primeval wisdom wherewith to foster the progress and education of humankind were not—like a modern philistine—fearful of receiving this wisdom from luciferic sources. They took upon themselves the obligation incumbent upon everyone to whom luciferic beings impart knowledge from spiritual realms. The obligation—for so it may be called, although such words do not always convey the exact meaning—was to use this luciferic, cosmic wisdom rightly, for the good of earth evolution. The difference between the "good" wisdom and the purely luciferic wisdom—which so far as *content* is concerned is exactly the same—is that the "good" wisdom is in hands other than those of the luciferic beings. That is the essential point. It is not a question of there being *one* wisdom that can be neatly packed away in some chamber of the soul and make a person virtuous! The wisdom of worlds is uniform, the only difference being whether it is in the hands of wise people who use it for good, whether it is in the hands of the Angeloi or Archangeloi, or whether it is in the hands of Lucifer and his hosts. In olden times the wisdom needed for the progress of humanity could be obtained only from a luciferic source; hence the initiates were obliged to receive it from that source and at the same time to take upon themselves the obligation not to yield to the aspirations of the luciferic beings.

Lucifer's intention was to convey the wisdom to humanity in such a way that it would induce people to abandon the path of earth evolution and take a path leading to a super-earthly sphere, a sphere aloof from the earth. The luciferic beings inculcated their wisdom into human beings but their desire was that it would make them turn away from the earth, without passing through earthly evolution. Lucifer wants to abandon the earth to its fate, to win humankind for a kingdom alien to the kingdom of Christ.

The sages of olden time who received the primeval wisdom from the hands of Lucifer had, as I said, to pledge themselves not to yield to his wishes but to use the wisdom for the good of earth evolution. And that, in essence, was what was accomplished through the pre-Christian Mysteries. If it be asked what it was that humanity received through these Mysteries, through the influence of the luciferic beings who, in post-Atlantean times, still inspired certain personalities like the Rishis of India and sent their messengers to the earth—the answer is that human beings received the rudiments of what has developed in the course of evolution into the faculties of speech and of thinking. Speaking and thinking are, in their origins, luciferic, but were drawn away from the grip of Lucifer by the sages of old. If you are really intent upon fleeing from Lucifer, then you must make up your minds to be dumb in the future, and not to think!

These things are part of the initiation science which must gradually come within the ken of humanity, although on account of the kind of education that has now been current for centuries in the civilized world, people shrink from such truths. The caricatured figure of Lucifer and Ahriman—the medieval devil—is constantly before their minds and they have been allowed to grow up in this philistine atmosphere for so long that even today they shudder at the thought of approaching treasures of wisdom that are intimately and deeply connected with evolution. It is much pleasanter to say: "If I protect myself from the devil, if I give myself to Christ with the simple-heartedness of a child, I shall be blessed, and my soul will find salvation." But in its deep foundations, human life is by no means such a simple matter. And it is essential for the future of human evolution that these things we are now discussing shall not be withheld. It must be known that the art of speaking and the art of thinking have become part of evolution only because they were received through the mediation of Lucifer. The luciferic element can still be observed in thinking. Speech, which has for long ages been differentiated and adapted to earthly needs, has already been assailed by Ahriman. It is he who has brought about different tongues on earth. Whereas the luciferic tendency is always toward unification, the fundamental tendency of the ahrimanic principle is differentiation. What would thinking be if it were not luciferic?

If thinking were not luciferic, human beings on the earth would be like one whose thought was utterly *non*-luciferic, namely Goethe. Goethe was one of those who, in a certain respect, deliberately set out to confront and defy the luciferic powers. That, however, makes it essential to keep constant hold of the concrete, individual reality. The moment you generalize or unify—at that moment you are nearing luciferic thinking. If you were to contemplate each human individual, each single plant, each single animal, each single stone in itself alone, having in mind the one, single object, not classifying into genera and species, not generalizing in your thought—then you would be little prone to luciferic thinking But anyone who was to attempt such a thing, even as a child, would never get beyond the lowest class in any modern school.

The fact of the matter is that the universal thinking implicit in pagan wisdom has gradually been exhausted. The human constitution is such that this luciferic principle of unification can no longer be of much real service to people on earth. This has been counteracted by the fact that the God-created nature of the human being has followed in the wake of earth evolution, has become related to, allied with the earth. And because this is so, through their own inherent nature, people are less allied with the luciferic element which always tends to draw them away from the earth.

But woe betide if humanity were simply to draw away from the luciferic element without putting something different in its place. That would bring nothing but evil. For then human beings would grow together with the earth, that is to say with the particular territory on earth where they are born; and cultural life would become completely specialized, completely differentiated. We can already see this tendency developing. It has taken root most markedly since the beginning of the nineteenth century; but the tendency to split up into smaller groups has been all too apparent as a result of the catastrophic world war. Chauvinism is more and more gaining the upper hand until it will finally lead people to split up to such an extent that at last a group will embrace only one single human being! Things could come to the point where individual human beings would again split into right and left, and be at war within themselves; left would be at loggerheads with right. Such tendencies are even now evident in the evolution of humankind. To combat this, a counterweight must be created; and this counterweight can only be created if, like the old wisdom inherent in paganism, a *new* wisdom, acquired by the free resolve and will of human beings, is infused into earthly culture. This new wisdom must again be an *Initiation wisdom.*

And here we come to a chapter that must not be withheld from modern knowledge. If, in the future, people were to do nothing themselves toward acquiring a new wisdom, then, without their consciousness, the whole of culture would become ahrimanic, and it would be easy for the influences issuing from Ahriman's incarnation to permeate all civilization on the earth. Precautions must therefore be taken in regard to the streams by which the ahrimanic form of culture is furthered. What would be the result if people were to follow the strong inclination they have today to let things drift on as they are, without understanding and guiding into right channels those streams which lead to an ahrimanic culture? As soon as Ahriman incarnates at the destined time in the West, the whole of culture would be impregnated with his forces. What else would come in his train? Through certain stupendous acts he would bring to humanity all the clairvoyant knowledge which until then can be acquired only by dint of intense labor and effort. People could live on as materialists, they could eat and drink—as much as may be left after the war!—and there would be no need for any spiritual efforts. The ahrimanic streams would continue their unimpeded course. When Ahriman incarnates in the West at the appointed time, he would establish a great occult school for the practice of magic arts of the greatest grandeur, and what otherwise can be acquired only by strenuous effort would be poured over humankind.

Let it never be imagined that Ahriman will appear as a kind of hoaxer, playing mischievous tricks on human beings. No, indeed! Lovers of ease who refuse to have anything to do with spiritual science would fall prey to his magic, for by means of these stupendous magic arts he would be able to make great numbers of human beings into seers—but in such a way that the clairvoyance of each individual would be strictly differentiated. What one person would see, a second and a third would not see. Confusion would prevail and in spite of being made receptive to clairvoyant wisdom, people would inevitably fall into strife on account of the sheer diversity of their visions. Ultimately, however, they would all be satisfied with their own particular vision, for each of them would be able to see into the spiritual world. In this way all culture on the earth would fall prey to Ahriman. Human beings would succumb to Ahriman simply through not having acquired by their own efforts what Ahriman is ready and able to give them. No more evil advice could be given than to say: "Stay just as you are! Ahriman will make all of you clairvoyant if you so desire. And you *will* desire it because Ahriman's power will be very great." But the result would be the establishment of Ahriman's kingdom on earth and the overthrow of everything achieved hitherto by human culture; all the disastrous tendencies unconsciously cherished by humankind today would take effect.

Our concern is that the wisdom of the future—a clairvoyant wisdom—shall be rescued from the clutches of Ahriman. Again let it be repeated that there is only *one* book of wisdom, not two kinds of wisdom. The issue is whether this wisdom is in the hands of Ahriman or of Christ. It cannot come into the hands of Christ unless people fight for it. And they can only fight for it by telling themselves that *by their own efforts* they must assimilate the content of spiritual science before the time of Ahriman's appearance on earth.

That, you see, is the cosmic task of spiritual science. It consists in preventing knowledge from becoming—or remaining—ahrimanic. A good way of playing into Ahriman's hands is to exclude everything of the nature of knowledge from denominational religion and to insist that simple faith is enough. If people cling to this simple faith, they condemn their soul to stagnation and then the wisdom that must be rescued from Ahriman cannot find entry. The point is not whether people do or do not simply receive the wisdom of the future but whether they work upon it; and those who do must take upon themselves the solemn duty of saving earthly culture for Christ, just as the ancient Rishis and initiates pledged themselves not to yield to Lucifer's proviso that humankind be enticed away from the earth.

The root of the matter is that for the wisdom of the future too, a struggle is necessary, a struggle similar to that waged against Lucifer by the ancient initiates through whose intermediary the faculties of speech and of thinking were transmitted to humanity. Just as it devolved upon the initiates of the primeval wisdom to wrest from Lucifer that which has become human reason, human intellect, so the insight which is to develop in the future into the inner realities of things must be wrested from the ahrimanic powers. Such are the issues—and these issues play strongly into life itself.

I recently read some notes written shortly before his death by one who was a friend of the anthroposophical movement. He had been wounded in the war and lay for a long time in hospital where, in the course of the operations performed on him, he had many a glimpse into the spiritual world. The last lines he wrote contain a remarkable passage, describing a vision which came to him not long before his death. In this last experience, the atmosphere around him became, as he expresses it, like dense granite, weighing upon his soul. Such an impression can be understood in the light of the knowledge that we have to battle for the wisdom of the future; for the ahrimanic powers do not allow this wisdom to be wrested from them without a struggle. Let it not be thought that wisdom can be attained through blissful visions. Real wisdom has to be acquired "in travail and suffering." What I have just told you about the dying man is a very good picture of such suffering, for in this struggle for the wisdom of the future, one of the most frequent experiences is that the world is pressing in upon us, as though the air had suddenly frozen into granite. It is possible to know why this is so. We have only to remember that it is the endeavor of the ahrimanic powers to reduce the earth to a state of complete rigidification. Their victory would be won if they succeeded in bringing earth, water, and air into this rigidified state. Were that to happen, the earth could not again acquire the Saturn warmth from which it proceeded and which must be regained in the Vulcan epoch; and to prevent this is the aim of the ahrimanic powers. A trend which has an important bearing on this is the lack of enthusiasm in human souls at the present time for the content of spiritual science. If this lack of enthusiasm were to persist, the first impulse toward the rigidification of the earth would emanate from human souls themselves, from their apathy, their indolence and love of ease. If you reflect that this rigidification is the aim of the ahrimanic powers, you will not be surprised that compression, the feeling that life is becoming granite-like, is one of the experiences that must be undergone in the struggle for the wisdom of the future.

But remember that people today can prepare themselves to look into the spiritual world by apprehending with their healthy human reason what spiritual science has to offer. The effort applied in study that lets itself be guided by healthy human reason can be part of the struggle which leads eventually to vision of the spiritual world. Many tendencies will have to be overcome, but for people of today the fundamental difficulty is that when they want to understand spiritual science they have to battle against their own granite-like skulls. If the human skull were less hard, less granite-like, spiritual science would be far more widely accepted at the present time. Infinitely more effective than any philistine avoidance of the ahrimanic powers would be to battle against Ahriman through sincere, genuine study of the content of spiritual science. For then human beings would gradually come to perceive spiritually the danger that must otherwise befall the earth physically, of being rigidified into granite-like density.

And so it must be emphasized that the wisdom of the future can be attained only through privations, travail, and pain; it must be attained by enduring the attendant sufferings of body and soul for the sake of the salvation of human evolution. Therefore the unwavering principle should be never to let oneself be deterred by suffering from the pursuit of this wisdom. So far as the external life of humankind is concerned, what is needed is that in the future the danger of the frozen rigidification—which, to begin with, would manifest in the moral sphere—shall be removed from the earth. But this can happen only if people envisage spiritually, feel inwardly and counter with their will, what would otherwise become physical reality.

At bottom, it is simply due to faint heartedness that people today are unwilling to approach spiritual science. They are not conscious of this, but it is so, nevertheless; they are fearful of the difficulties that will have to be encountered on every hand. When people come to spiritual science they so often speak of the need for "upliftment." By this they usually mean a sense of comfort and inner well-being. But that cannot be offered, for it would simply lull them into stupor and draw them away from the light they need. What is essential is that from now onward, knowledge of the driving forces of evolution must not be withheld from humankind. It must be realized that in very truth the human being is balanced as it were between the luciferic and the ahrimanic powers, and that the Christ has become a companion of human beings, leading them, first away from the battle with Lucifer, and then into the battle with Ahriman.

The evolution of humanity must be understood in the light of these facts. One who presents secrets of cosmic existence in the way that must be done in spiritual science is often laughed to scorn, for example about the use of the principle of the number *seven*—as you will find in my book *Theosophy*. But you will notice that people do not laugh when the rainbow is described as sevenfold, or the scale—tonic, second, third, and so on, up to the octave which is a repetition of the tonic. In the physical world these things are accepted, but not when it comes to the spiritual. What must be regained here is something that was implicit in the old pagan wisdom. A last glimmer of this pagan wisdom in regard to a matter like the principle of the number seven is to be found in the Pythagorean school—which was actually a Mystery school. You can read about Pythagoras today in any text book; but you will never find any understanding of the reason why he based the world order on number. The reason was because in the ancient wisdom everything was based on number. And a last glimmer of insight into the wisdom contained in numbers still survived when Pythagoras founded his school. Other branches of the ancient wisdom survived much longer, some indeed until the sixth and seventh centuries of the Christian era. Up to that time many true things about the higher worlds are said in the sphere of what is called natural philosophy. And then, gradually, this primeval intelligence in humankind ran dry—if I may use this expression.

Let us picture some orthodox representative of modern learning sitting in a corner and saying: "What nonsense these anthroposophists talk! What do they mean by asserting that the primeval wisdom has run dry? Wonderful, epoch-making results have been achieved, above all during the last few centuries, and are still being achieved. There may have been a temporary halt in 1914, but at any rate up to then marvels were accomplished!" But if you look candidly and without bias at what has been achieved most recently, you will arrive at the following conclusion. Admittedly, masses of notes have been collected—masses of scientific and historical data. This kind of collecting has become the fashion. Countless experiments have been made and described. But now ask yourselves: Are there any fundamentally *new* ideas in all that this modern age has produced? New ideas, new conceptions *were* given by individual spirits like Goethe—but Goethe has not been understood. If you study recent findings of natural science or historical research, it will be clear to you that, with respect to *ideas*, there is nothing new. Certainly, Darwin made journeys, described many things he saw on these journeys and gathered it all into an idea. But if you grasp the idea of evolution in its details, *as idea*, you will find it in the Greek philosopher Anaxagoras. So too you will find the fundamental principles of modern natural science in Aristotle—that is to say in the pre-Christian era. These ideas are treasures of the primeval wisdom—springing from a luciferic source. But the primeval wisdom has run dry, and something new in the form of insight into the spiritual world must be attained. A certain willingness on the part of humanity is necessary to undertake the labor entailed by really new ideas. And humankind today is sorely in need of new ideas, especially concerning the realm and the life of the soul. Fundamentally, all that science tells us in regard to the soul amounts to nothing more than a collection of words. What is taught in the lecture halls about thinking, feeling, and willing is simply a matter of words thrown out spasmodically. It amounts to little more than the sounds of the words. There is hardly the beginning of an attempt to take seriously anything that is really new.

In this connection one may have curious experiences! Some time ago I was invited to speak to a "Schopenhauer Society" in Dresden. I thought to myself: Yes—a Schopenhauer society—that must surely be something out of the ordinary! So I tried to show how the contrast between sleeping and waking, between waking up and going to sleep is to be understood in the psychological sense, how the *soul* is involved. I spoke of something I have recently mentioned to you, namely, that a zero-point is there at the moments of falling asleep and waking up, that sleep is not merely a cessation of the waking state, but bears the same relation to the waking state as debts bear to assets.

If you were to search through modern psychology you would not find the slightest trace of any attempt to get to the root of these far-reaching matters. After the lecture, in a "discussion" as it was called, certain learned members of the audience got up to speak. One of these philosophers made a really splendid statement, to the following effect. He said: "What we have been hearing could not possibly be a concern of serious science. Serious science has other, very different matters with which to occupy itself.We can know nothing of what has just been put before us so plausibly; none of it is a corcern of human cognition. Moreover we have known it all for a long time." In other words, therefore: what we cannot know is something with which we have long been familiar!

Now contradictions do exist, but contradictions of this kind exist only in the heads of present-day scholars! If someone says that certain things cannot be known, that they are not objects of human cognition—well and good, that is his opinion. But if he says in the same breath that he has known all about them for a long time, then there is an obvious contradiction. Erudite scholars of today often have a habit of placing two diametrically opposite opinions side by side in this way.

This kind of thinking has a great deal to do with the present situation. An individual—thanks to the Divine Powers and also, be it remembered, to Lucifer and Ahriman—is often able to form a fairly sound judgment of these things; but when it comes to presenting them to the world—that is a different matter altogether. Many people are willing to embark upon the study of spiritual science provided they find a society of rather sectarian tendencies in which they can take refuge. But when they have to face the world and present something of which the world itself possesses evidence, everything is apt to go up in smoke and they become veritable philistines. And then Ahriman's progress is greatly furthered.

I WANT TO SPEAK TODAY OF something that will help to deepen our understanding of truths that must now be given to humankind by anthroposophy. We have often spoken of the two poles of forces of the human being: the pole of will and the pole of intelligence. To understand the nature of the human being we must be constantly mindful of these two poles.

The human is a being of will and a being of intelligence. Between them—at any rate from birth until death—lies the element of feeling, constituting the bridge between the intelligence and the will. You know that these forces separate from each other in a certain sense when people reach what is called the threshold of the spiritual world.

Our study today will be concerned more particularly with the relationship in which humanity stands to the surrounding world, on the one side as a being of intelligence and on the other as a being of will. We shall deal with the latter first.

In the life between birth and death, human beings unfold the force of will as the impulse of their actions and activity. As it comes to expression through the human organism, the force of will is a very intricate, complicated matter. Nevertheless in one aspect, everything of the nature of human will bears a great likeness, amounting almost to identity, with certain forces of nature. It is therefore quite correct to speak of an inner relation between the forces of will in the human being and the forces of nature.

You know from earlier studies that even while people are awake, they are in a condition resembling sleep wherever their will is involved. True, we have in our consciousness the ideas lying behind what we will, but *how* a particular idea takes effect in the form of will—of that we know nothing. We do not know how the idea, "I move my arm," is connected with the process leading to the actual movement of the arm. This process lies entirely in the subconscious and it may truly be said that people are no more conscious of the real process of will than they are of what takes place during sleep. But when the question arises as to the connection of human will with the surrounding world, we come to something that will strike the kind of consciousness that has developed in the course of the last three to five centuries as highly paradoxical. It is generally thought that the evolution of the earth would be the same even if human beings had no part in it at all. A typical natural scientist describes the evolution of the earth as a series, let us say, of geological, purely physical processes. And even if scientists do not expressly say so, they have in mind that from the earth's beginning until its hypothetical end, everything would go on just the same even if it were uninhabited by human beings. Why is this view held by natural science today? The reason is that when anything takes place, for example in the mineral kingdom, or the plant kingdom, let us say on November 9, 1919, people believe that its cause lies in what has happened in the mineral kingdom prior to this particular point of time. People think: the mineral kingdom takes its course and what happens at any point is the effect of what went before; the mineral effect is due to a mineral cause.

This is the way people think and you will find evidence of it in any text book of geology. Conditions obtaining at the present time are said to be the effects of the Ice Age, or of some preceding epoch—but the causes are attributed entirely to what once took place in the mineral kingdom as such; the fact that *humanity* inhabits the earth is ignored. The belief is that even were humans not present, everything would run a similar course, that the external reality would be the same—although, in fact, humankind has always been part of this external reality. The truth is that the earth is one whole, humanity itself being one of the active factors in the earth's evolution. I will give you an example.

You know that our present epoch—thinking of it for the moment in the wider sense, as comprising the period since the great Atlantean catastrophe—was preceded by the Atlantean epoch itself, when the continents of Europe, Africa, and America in their present form were not in existence. At that time there was one main continent on the earth—Atlantis as it is called—extending over the area that is now the Atlantic Ocean. You know too that at a certain period in this Atlantean evolution, immorality of a particular kind was rampant throughout the then-civilized world. Human beings had far greater power over the forces of nature than they later possessed and employed these forces for evil purposes. Thus we can look back to an age of widespread immorality. And then came the great Atlantean catastrophe. The orthodox geologist will naturally trace this catastrophe to processes in the mineral kingdom; indeed it is a fact that one part of the earth subsided and another arose. But it will not occur to those who base their thinking on the principles of modern natural science to say to themselves that the deeds and activities of human beings were among the contributory causes. Yet so it is. In very truth the Atlantean catastrophe was the outcome of the deeds of people on the earth.

Outer, mineral causes are not alone responsible for these great catastrophic events that break in upon earth existence. We must look for causes lying within the sphere of human actions and impulses. Humanity itself belongs to the chain of causative forces in earth existence. Nor does this apply only to an event of such magnitude but to what is happening all the time. Only the connection between what goes on within human beings and cosmic happenings which take effect in tellurian events remains hidden, to begin with. In this respect the whole of our natural science amounts to a great, all-embracing illusion. For

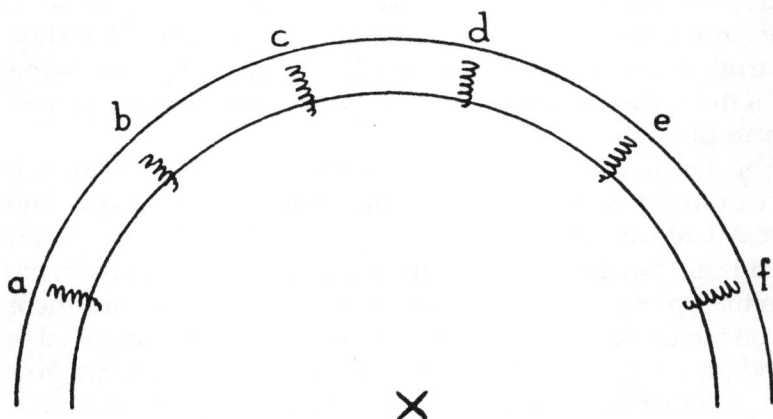

if you want to get at the real causes you will not discover them by studying the mineral, plant, and animal kingdoms alone.

Let me give you the following illustration of what comes into consideration here. We will approach it, so to speak, from the opposite side. Here (X) is the center of the earth. When something takes place in the mineral kingdom, the plant kingdom, or the animal kingdom, it is a matter of seeking the causes. The causes lie at certain points which are to be found everywhere. You can picture what I mean by thinking of the following. In the region around Naples in Italy, you will find that the earth over a wide area will emit vapor if you take a piece of paper and set it alight. Vapors begin to rise from the ground beneath you. You will say: the force which drives up the vapors lies in the physical process generated by the lighting of the paper. In this case, the physical process is that by lighting the paper you rarify the air and because of the rarification of the air the vapors inside the earth press upward. They are kept down by the normal air-pressure and this is diminished by setting light to the paper. If I merely want to give an example of effects of a purely mineral nature—such as these vapors arising out of the earth—I could say for the sake of illustration that here, and here (points in the diagram), a piece of paper is set alight. This shows you that the causes of the rising of the vapor do not lie

below the soil, but above it. Now these points in the diagram—
a, b, c, d, e, f—do not represent pieces of paper that have been
set alight; in this instance they represent something different.
Imagine, to begin with, that each point on its own has no significance but that the significance lies in the system of points as a
whole. Do not think now of the pieces of lighted paper, but of
something else which at the moment I will not specify. Something else is there as an active cause, above the surface of the
earth; and these different causes do not work singly, but
together. And now imagine that there are not six points only,
but, let us say, 1,500 million points[1] all working together, producing a combined effect. These 1,500 million points are actually there. Each of you has within you what may be called the
center of gravity of your own physical structure. When people
are awake, this center of gravity lies just below the diaphragm;
when they are asleep it lies a little lower. There are therefore
some 1,500 million of these centers of gravity spread over the
earth, producing a combined effect. And what issues from this
combined effect is the actual cause of a great deal of what takes
place in the mineral, plant, and animal kingdoms on the earth.
It is a scientific fallacy to trace back to mineral causes the forces
manifesting in air and water and in the mineral realm; in reality
the causes are to be found *within the human beings.*

This is a truth of which there is scarcely an inkling today. It
is known to very, very few that the causes of processes active in
the mineral, plant, and animal kingdoms lie within the human
organism. (This does not apply to all the forces working in
these kingdoms of nature, but to a large proportion of them.)
Within humankind lie the causes for what happens on earth.
Therefore mineralogy, botany, zoology, cannot be cultivated
truly without anthropology—without the study of the human
being. Science tells us of physical, chemical, and mechanical
forces. These forces are intimately connected with the human
will, *with the force of human will that is concentrated in our center of*

---

1. Representing, approximately, the total population of the earth.

gravity. If we speak of the earth with an eye to the truth of these matters, we must not follow the geologist in speaking of an earth in the abstract, but humanity must be accounted an integral part of the earth. These are the truths that reveal themselves on yonder side of the threshold. Everything that can be known on this side of the threshold belongs to the realm of the illusions of knowledge, not to the realm of truth.

At this point the question arises: What relation is there between the forces of will that are concentrated in our center of gravity, and the external, physical, and chemical forces? We are speaking, remember, of present-day humanity. In normal life, this relation takes effect in the metabolic processes. When people take into themselves the substances of the outer world, it is their will that actually digests and works upon these substances. And if nothing else were in operation, then what is taken into the organism from outside would simply be destroyed. The human will has the power to dissolve and destroy all extraneous substances and forces; and the relation between the human being and the mineral, plant, and animal kingdoms of nature today is such that our will is connected with the forces of dissolution and destruction inherent in our planet.

We could not live were this destruction not to take place— but for all that it *is* destruction. This must never be forgotten. And what are often described as unlawful magical practices are based essentially on the fact that certain human beings learn to employ their will wrongfully, in such a way that they do not confine the destructive forces to their normal operations within the organism but extend them over other human beings, deliberately and consciously applying the forces of destruction that are anchored in their will. That, quite obviously, is a practice that is never, under any circumstances, permissible.

Through our will we are connected with the earth's forces of decline. And if as human beings we had only our forces of will, the earth would be condemned through us, through humankind, to sheer destruction. The prospect of the future would then be far from inspiring; it would be a vista of the gradual dissolution of the earth and its ultimate dispersal in cosmic space. So much for the one pole in the human constitution.

But the human is a twofold being. One pole is, as we have seen, connected with the destructive forces of our planet; the other pole—that of intelligence—is connected with the will by the bridge of feeling. But in waking life, human intelligence is of little account as far as the planet earth is concerned. During waking life we cannot really establish a true relationship to earth existence through our intelligence. What I have told you in regard to the will happens while we are awake, although we are not conscious of it. If you see a rock crumbling away and ask where the actual causes of the crumbling lie, then you must look into the inner, organic nature of the human being. Strange as this will seem to the modern mind, it is indeed so. But as I said, the earth would face a sorry future if the other pole of human nature were not there—the pole of the upbuilding forces. Just as the causes of all destruction lie in the will that is concentrated in our center of gravity, so the upbuilding forces lie in the sphere into which we pass during sleep. From the time of falling asleep until that of waking, we are in a condition figuratively described by saying that with our "I" and astral body we are outside the physical body. But then we are entirely beings of soul and spirit, unfolding the forces that are in operation between falling asleep and waking. During this time we are connected, through these forces, with everything that builds up the earth planet, everything that adds to the forces of destruction the constructive, upbuilding forces. If you did not go about the earth, the destructive forces actually proceeding from your will would not be working in the mineral, plant, and animal kingdoms. If you never went to sleep, the forces whereby the earth is continually upbuilt would not stream out of your intelligence. The constructive, upbuilding forces of the planet earth also lie in humanity itself. I do *not* say: in the individual human being—for I have expressly said that all these single causes form a collective whole. The upbuilding forces lie in humankind as a whole, actually in the pole of intelligence in our being but *not* in our waking intelligence. Waking intelligence is really like a lifeless entity thrusting itself into earth evolution. The intelligence that works, unconsciously, during our sleep—that is what builds up the earth planet. By this I am only trying to explain that it is a fallacy to look outside the human being for the destructive and the constructive forces of our earth; you must look for them *within* the human being. Once you grasp this, what I am now going to say will not be unintelligible.

You look up to the stars, saying that something is streaming from them that can be perceived by human sense organs here on earth. But what you behold when you gaze at the stars is not of the same nature as what you perceive on the earth in the mineral, plant, and animal kingdoms. In reality it proceeds from *beings of intelligence and will* whose life is bound up with those stars. The effects appear to be physical because the stars are at a distance. They are not in reality physical at all. What you actually see are the inner activities of beings of will and intelligence in the stars. I have already spoken to you of the ingenious description of the sun given by astrophysicists. But if it were possible to journey to the sun by some means of transport invented by a Jules Verne, it would be found with amazement that nothing of what was to be expected from these physical descriptions exists. The descriptions are merely a composite picture of solar phenomena. What we see is in reality the working of will and intelligence which *at a distance appears as light.* If inhabitants of the moon—supposing in this sense there were such beings—were to look at the earth, they would not detect its grassy or mineral surfaces but—also perceiving it as a light effect or something similar—they would detect what takes place around the centers of gravity of human bodies and also the effects of the conditions in which human beings live between going to sleep and waking. That is what would actually be seen from the universe. Even the most perfect instrument would not enable the chairs, for instance, on which you are now sitting, to be seen; what would be seen is all that is taking place in the region of your centers of gravity and what would happen if you were suddenly to fall asleep—it is to be hoped that this would not happen in every case! But wherever it did happen, it would be perceived out in the universe.

So that to the outer universe, what takes place *through human beings* is the perceptible reality—not what surrounds us in earthly existence. A very common saying is that everything perceived with the senses is maya—the great illusion—no reality but simply appearance. Such an abstraction is of little account. It has meaning only when one enters into the concrete, as we have now been doing. To say glibly that the animal, plant, and mineral worlds are maya means nothing. What *is* of value is the realization that what you perceive outwardly depends fundamentally upon yourselves and that—not of course at each moment but in the course of human evolution—you make yourselves an integral part of the chain of causes and effects.

Even when such a shattering truth is uttered—and I think it may well be shattering—it is not always seen in the aspect where it becomes of importance in life. Such a truth assumes importance only when we perceive its consequences. We are not physical beings only; we are moral—or maybe immoral—beings in earthly existence. What we do is determined by impulses of a moral nature.

Now just think with what bitter doubt modern thought is assailed in this domain. Natural science provides a knowledge of the earthly that is confined to the connection between purely external causes and effects; and in this cycle of natural causes and effects, the human being too is involved. So it is alleged by external, abstract science which takes account of one aspect only of earthly existence.

The fact that moral impulses also light up in people is admitted but nothing is known about the connection between these moral impulses and what comes to pass in the round of external nature. Indeed the dilemma of modern philosophy is that the philosophers hear on the one hand from the scientists that everything is involved in a chain of natural causes and effects—and on the other hand have to admit that moral impulses light up in people. That is the reason why Kant wrote two "Critiques": the *Critique of Pure Reason*, concerned with the relation of the human being to a purely natural course of things, and the *Critique of Practical Reason* where he puts forward his moral postulates—which in truth, if I may speak figuratively, hover in the air, come out of the blue and have no *a priori* relation with natural causes.

As long as we believe that what takes place in the external manifestations of nature can be traced only to similar manifestations, as long as we cling to this illusion, the intervention of moral impulses is something that remains separate and apart from the course of nature. Nearly everything that is discussed today lies under the shadow of this breach. In their thinking people cannot fuse the earthly round as such with the moral life of humanity. But as soon as you grasp something of what I have tried briefly to outline, you will be able to say: Yes, as a human being I am a unity, and moral impulses are alive within me. They live in what I am as a physical being. But as a physical human being I am fundamentally the cause—together with all humankind—of every physical happening. The moral conduct and achievements of human beings on the earth are the real causes of what comes to pass in the course of earth existence.

Natural history and natural science describe the earth in the way we find in text books of geology, botany, and so forth. What is said there seems entirely satisfactory according to the premises formed through modern education. But let us suppose that an inhabitant of Mars were to come down to the earth and observe it in the light of *Martian* premises. I am not saying that such a thing could happen but merely trying to illustrate what I mean. Suppose a being from Mars, having wandered dumbly about the earth were then to learn some human language, read some geology, and thus discover what kind of ideas prevail concerning the processes and happenings on the earth. This being would say: But that is not *all*. By far the most important factor is ignored. For example, I have noticed crowds of students loitering about in their beer houses, drinking and indulging their passions. Something is happening there: the human will is working in the metabolism. These are processes of which no mention is made in your books on physics and geology; they contain no reference to the fact that the course of earth existence is also affected by whether the students drink or do not drink. That is what a being not entirely immersed in earthly ideas and prejudices would find lacking in the descriptions given by human beings themselves of happenings on earth. For a being from Mars there would be no question but that moral impulses, pervading human deeds and the whole of human life, are part and parcel of the course of nature. According to modern preconceptions there is something inexorable in the play of nature, indeed pleasantly inexorable for materialistic thinkers. They imagine that the earth's course would be exactly the same were no human beings in existence; that whether they behave decently or not makes no fundamental difference or really alters anything. But that is not the case! The all-essential causes of what happens on the earth do not lie outside the human being; they lie *within humankind*. And if earthly consciousness is to expand to cosmic consciousness, humanity must realize that the earth—not over short but over long stretches of time—is made in its own likeness, in the likeness of humanity itself. There is no better means of lulling people to sleep than to impress upon them that they have no share in the course taken by earth existence. This narrows down human responsibility to the single individual, the single personality.

The truth is that the responsibility for the course of earth existence through ages of cosmic time, lies with humanity. Everyone must feel themselves to be a member of humanity, the earth itself being the body for that humanity.

Someone may say: For ten years I have given way to my passions, indulged my fancies and have thereby ruined my body. With equal conviction such a person should be able to say: If earthly humanity follows impure moral impulses, then the body of the earth will be different from what it would be were the moral impulses pure. The day-fly, because it lives for twenty-four hours only, has a view of the world differing entirely from that of human beings. The range of our vision is not wide enough to perceive that what happens externally in the course of nature is not dependent upon purely natural causes. In regard to the present configuration of Europe, it is far more important to ask what manner of life prevailed among human beings in the civilized world two thousand years ago than to investigate the external mineral and plant structure of the earth. The destiny of our physical earth planet in another two thousand years will not depend upon the present constitution of our mineral world, but upon what we do and allow to be done. With world consciousness, human responsibility widens into world responsibility. With such consciousness we feel as we look up to the starry heavens that we are responsible to this cosmic expanse, permeated and pervaded as it is by spirit—that we are responsible to this world for how we conduct the earth. We grow together with the cosmos in concrete reality when behind the phenomena we seek for the truth.

I so often tell you that we must learn to perceive the concrete realities of things for the most part taught as abstractions today. Nothing much is accomplished by adopting oriental traditions such as: the external world of the senses is maya. We must go much deeper if we are to arrive at the truth. Such abstractions do not carry us far, because in the form in which they have been handed down they are nothing but the sediment of a primeval wisdom that did not hover in abstractions but teemed with concrete realities which must be brought to light again through spiritual intuition and research. When you read in oriental literature of maya and of truth as its antithesis, do not imagine that what you read there today can be really intelligible to you. It is only a much later compilation of matters that were concrete realities to the ancient wisdom. We must get back to these concrete realities. People think today that they have some understanding of cosmic processes when they assert that the external world of sense is maya. But nothing can be understood unless one presses on to the underlying realities. The moment it is realized: we have not to ask how the present mineral world has developed out of the mineral processes of another age; we have rather to ask about what has been going on in humankind—at that moment the real meaning of the saying, "the outer world is maya," becomes clear. Then we begin to perceive in the human being a reality far greater than is usually perceived. And then the feeling of responsibility for earth existence begins.

If you will try to get to the inner core of these things—and it must be by inward contemplation, not by means of the kind of intelligence employed in natural science—you will gradually find your way to the realization that humankind is composed of *free* human beings. Nature does not, in truth, counteract our freedom, for as human beings we ourselves fashion the nature immediately surrounding us. It is only in its partial manifestations that nature counteracts our freedom. Nature counteracts our freedom to an extent no greater than if—to give an example—you are stretching out your hand and someone else takes hold of it and checks the movement. You will not deny freedom of will simply because someone else checks a movement. As people of the present day we are checked in many respects because of some action of our predecessors that is only now taking effect. But at all events it was an action of *human beings.*— What human beings? Not anyone against whom we can turn with reproach, for we ourselves were the ones who, in earlier earthly lives, brought about the conditions obtaining today.

We must not confine ourselves to the mere mention of repeated earthly lives but think of the connection between them in such a way that even in external nature we perceive the effects of causes we ourselves laid down in earlier lives. Naturally, in reference to the single, individual human being, we must speak of contributory causes only, for in all these things, as I have said, it is a matter of the collective interworking of human beings on the earth. None of us should, for that reason, exclude ourselves as individuals, for each of us has a share in what is brought about by humanity as a whole and then comes to expression in what constitutes the body for the whole of earthly humanity in its onflowing life.

I have been endeavoring to give you an idea of how a spiritual scientist must regard the statements made in ordinary scientific text-books. Suppose I were to draw a series of figures:

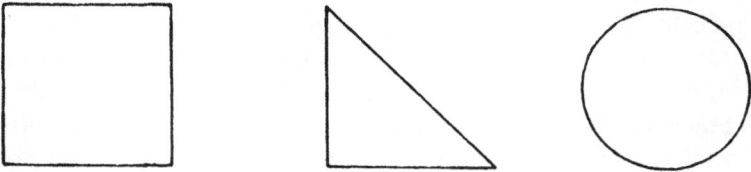

And now suppose some creature who had never lived in our world were to crawl out of the earth and, having some rudiments of arithmetical knowledge, were to look at the figures and say: First figure, second figure, third figure. The third is the effect of the second, and the second the effect of the first. Effect of the first figure—a triangle; effect of the second—a circle. This creature would then be combining cause and effect. But it would be a fallacy, for I have drawn each figure separately. In reality the one is independent of the other. It only *appears* to be dependent to this creature who associates what comes first with what follows, as if the one were the outcome of the other. This, approximately, is how the geologist describes the process of the earth: Diluvial epoch, Tertiary epoch, Quaternary epoch, and so on. But this is no more true than the statement that the circle is the outcome, the effect of the triangle, or the triangle the effect of the rectangular figure. The configurations of the earth are brought about autonomously—through the deeds of earthly humanity, including the mysterious workings of the intelligence during the periods of sleep when human beings are outside their physical bodies.

This shows you that the descriptions given by external science are very largely illusion—maya. But merely to speak about maya is of little account. To the assertion that the external world is maya we must be able to reply by stating where the actual causes lie. These causes are hidden to a great extent from our powers of cognition. The part played by humankind in shaping earth existence cannot be fathomed by means of external science but only by an inner science. My book *Knowledge of the Higher Worlds and Its Attainment* speaks of the human being's inner activity between the time of going to sleep and waking. This can be revealed by knowledge that reaches down to the sphere of the *will*. Human beings know nothing of the connection between the will and the outer world for the processes of the will are hidden and concealed. We do not know what is really going on when by lifting our hand we set in operation a process of will; nor do we know that this process continues and has an effect in the whole course of earth existence.

This is indicated in the scene in my mystery play, *The Portal of Initiation*, where the actions of Capesius and Strader have their outcome in cosmic manifestations—in thunder and lightning. It is, of course, a pictorial representation, but the picture contains a deeper truth; it is not fantasy but actual truth. For a fairly long period in evolution, truths of this kind have been voiced only by true poets whose fantasy must always be perception of supersensible processes.

This is very little understood by modern people who like to relegate poetry, indeed all art, to a place separate and apart from external reality. They feel relieved not to be asked to see in poetry anything more than fantasy. True poetry, true art, is of course, no more than a reflection of supersensible truth— but a reflection it is. Even if poets are not themselves conscious of the supersensible happenings, if their soul is linked with the cosmos, if they have not been torn away from the cosmos by materialistic education, they give utterances to supersensible truths, in spite of having to express them in pictures drawn from the world of sense.

Many examples of this are contained in the second part of Goethe's *Faust*, where as I have shown in the case of particular passages, the imagery has a direct relation with supersensible processes.[1] The development of art in recent centuries affords evidence of what I have been saying. Take any picture painted by no means very long ago, and you will find that as a rule, landscape is given very secondary importance. The painting of landscape has come into prominence only since the last three to five centuries. Earlier than that you will find that landscape takes second place; it is the *human* world that is brought to the forefront because the consciousness still survived that in regard to objective processes of earth existence the human world is much more important than the landscape—which is but the effect of the human world. In the very birth of preference for landscape there lies, in the sphere of art, the parallel phenomenon of the birth of the materialistic trend of mind—consisting in the belief that landscape and what it represents has an existence of its own, entirely apart from humanity. But the truth is quite the reverse. Were some inhabitant of Mars to come down to the earth he would certainly be able to see meaning in Leonardo da Vinci's "Last Supper," but not in paintings of landscapes. He would see landscapes—including painted landscapes—and the whole configuration of the earth quite differently and with his particular organ of sense could not fathom their meaning. Please remember that I am saying these things merely in order to illustrate hypothetically what I want to convey.

So you see, the saying: "the external world is maya" cannot be fully understood without entering into the concrete realities. But to do this we must relate ourselves intimately with earth existence as a whole, know ourselves to be an integral part of it.

---

1. Twenty-eight lectures given in the year 1915. *Geisteswissenschaftliche Erlauterungen zu Goethe's Faust.*

And then we must grasp the thought that there can be external and apparent realities which are not the truth, not the true realities. If you have a rose in your room, it is an *apparent* reality only, for the rose as it is in front of you there cannot be the reality. It can be true reality only while it is growing on the rose tree, united with the roots which in turn are united with the earth. The earth as described by the geologists is as little a true reality as a plucked rose is a reality.

Spiritual science endeavors never to halt at the untrue reality, but always to seek what must be added, in order to have the *whole*, true reality. The meager sense of reality prevailing in our present civilization expresses itself in the very fact that every external manifestation is taken as reality. But there is reality only in what lies before one as an integrated whole. The earth by itself, without human beings, is no more a true reality than the rose plucked from the rose tree. These things must be pondered and worked upon; they must not remain theories but pass over into our feelings. We must feel ourselves members of the whole earth. It is of importance again and again to call up the thoughts: this finger on my hand has true reality only as long as it is part of my organism; if it is cut off it no longer has true reality. Similarly, the human being has no true reality apart from the earth, nor has the earth without humankind. It is an unreal concept when modern scientific investigators think, according to their premises, that earth evolution would run the same course if humanity were not there. I recently showed you that it would not be so, by telling you that the bodies laid aside by human beings at death become a leaven in earth evolution and that if no human bodies—either by burial or cremation—became part of the earth, the whole course of physical happenings would be other than it is in consequence of these bodies having been received into the earth.

In the lecture today I wanted to speak in greater detail of the connection between the two poles of will and intelligence in human beings and their cosmic environment.

www.ingramcontent.com/pod-product-compliance
Lightning Source LLC
Chambersburg PA
CBHW032025090426
42741CB00006B/739